one-day room makeovers

How to Get the Designer Look for Less with Three Easy Steps

martin amado

Design Expert, TV Host and Owner of The WOW Factor!, Inc.

PAGE STREET
PUBLISHING CO.

PAGE STREET
PUBLISHING CO.

First published in 2018 by
Page Street Publishing Co.
27 Congress Street, Suite 105
Salem, MA 01970

www.pagestreetpublishing.com

Distributed by Macmillan, sales in Canada by The Canadian Manda Group.

22   21   20   19   18   1   2   3   4   5

ISBN-13: 978-1-62414-536-0
ISBN-10: 1-62414-536-1

Library of Congress Control Number: 2018930896

Cover and book design by Page Street Publishing Co.
Photography by Venjhamin Reyes
Photographs on pages 5 (middle), 122–123, 124 (right), 126, 128 (right) and 129 (left) by Hector Torres
Illustrations by Andrea Centeno

Printed and bound in China

I would like to dedicate this book in loving memory of my grandmother, Norma Fabelo Cue Sosa, who taught me by example that it was better to give than to receive and who always put her family first. She showed me the meaning of unconditional love, and it was a privilege for me to be her grandson. You are always with me, and everything I accomplish I owe to you. I love you, Abuela.

Contents

Introduction
The Connection Between Home & Heart Matters

A home should be a reflection of you and your personal style, and I believe it should tell a story about the people that live there. But what if the story or first impression you're telling is not a true representation of who you are and you don't even realize it? This would be the equivalent of walking around wearing a mask since people can't see the real you behind the disguise either. Sounds silly, I know, but take a moment to look around your home and see if the spaces really capture your spirit and personality. Chances are you might be giving more thought to how you coordinate your outfit every morning than what your home's décor is saying about you.

As a designer, I believe that when your surroundings are at odds with your inner self, you're living in an environment of conflict; unconsciously in one form or another, it could be holding you back from living a better life. The good news is that there is help. When you achieve that balance whereby your exterior space mirrors who you are on the inside, a new world will open up. Your outlook on life, love and happiness will improve. Coming home after a long day at work will take on a whole new meaning; you'll invite friends over for company more often; and even more importantly, you'll be comfortable and happy just doing nothing in your home because you've created your own perfect haven.

Through my work as a designer, I've come across this conflict between style and self so many times that I decided to share my insight through the room makeovers in this book . . . a journal full of decorating tips that will inspire you to design the life you wish to live. No, this is not a self-help book, but I guess you can consider me a design doctor, a therapist of sorts. I have to use my intuition to analyze and tap into what a homeowner truly wants their home to become when they hire my services. I've met many homeowners who have vibrant personalities, yet they choose to live with white, boring walls; others settle for a mismatch of furniture styles they don't like simply because they don't know what they do want. I find all these contradictions fascinating. In the end, it's my job to make sense of this and assist them in making their vision for their home a reality, so that it reflects their true self. When that connection happens, the transformation truly transcends the physical makeover of the space . . . it can literally change your life!

Decorating is not about making a space within four walls look as if it belongs in a designer magazine. It's about creating an experience that appeals to your senses when you walk into a room and that captures the best of you. Ultimately, you'll find it will inspire you in other areas of your life—you can't help it. You'll have a newly found sense of pride in your surroundings and a renewed confidence in yourself. The best part is you don't have to spend a fortune to achieve this blissful medium between home and heart. You can also find joy in the little things such as lighting a candle, placing fresh flowers in a vase or wrapping yourself in a cozy throw while watching television. These are the simplest pleasures you can do to nurture your spirit and create lasting memories in your home.

Did you ever think interior decorating can make such a difference? I invite you to experience it with this book, featuring real designs for real people. In it, I take you into my world where I transform rooms in one day to give them a decorator look for less. This is second nature to me because I can visualize the essence of a room and what it can become as soon as I see it. I realize not everyone has this gift, so I want to demystify the decorating process by sharing my three steps to decorating a room to help you understand how I approach every design project. It's not about how much money you have to decorate, but what you do with it to make an impact in your space. Going forward, I use the term homeowners, but my advice can apply in most circumstances to renters as well.

I'm so grateful to the many families I've met through my business and work on television who granted me access into their personal spaces. The most rewarding part has been watching their faces when their room makeovers are revealed. That moment is priceless and stays with me forever. It's my motivation to continue doing what I do and the inspiration behind this book because I want everyone to experience that feeling of happiness with their home, too.

On a more personal level, there comes a point in your life where you might question your purpose in the world and how you can make a difference—at least, I did. As I look back at the direction my career path has taken and my journey to get to where I am today, I realize I am making a difference in people's lives through my work, one room at a time. This is my purpose at this moment in time, and I'm so blessed I was chosen to do this. It's a privilege I try not to take for granted.

Thank you for your trust, for allowing me to do what I love and share my passion with you.

a.k.a. The Makeover Maestro

Meet Martin Amado
How I Became Known as the Makeover Maestro Doing One-Day Makeovers

Thanks for picking up this book! I'm Martin Amado, a design and lifestyle expert based in South Florida, which is where I was born and raised. Some of you may be familiar with my work on television doing what I do best: transforming spaces in one day on a budget. I have a passion for decorating, and I truly believe that everyone deserves to live in a beautiful home. For me, decorating is not just about making a space look beautiful; it's about creating an environment that has a "wow factor" and reflects your personal style.

Between my television projects and private clients, I've worked on too many makeovers to keep count; but trust me when I say that I've seen it all—the good, the bad and everything in between when it comes to home décor. What I know is that, no matter how big or small your design disaster, every space has the potential to look great without breaking the bank. My goal with this book is to share with you all my designer secrets, room by room, to help you create the home of your dreams and avoid costly mistakes. I want you to consider me as your personal "take-home decorator" throughout this process—whether you're a first-time homeowner starting from scratch or are looking for ideas to refresh your current home.

Had you asked me over 25 years ago if I'd be an interior decorator, let alone working on television as such, the answer would've been no. I've always been a very creative person and remember as a teenager rearranging my bedroom and redecorating it often, but it never occurred to me at such a young age that I could make a business out of it. I knew I liked it just as much as I did acting; however, raised in a Hispanic household where my abuela was a great influence, she hinted at more financially stable careers like becoming a doctor or lawyer.

As a kid, the Universe was already preparing me for the path I would be on today. My dad was a painting contractor, and on the weekends I would go to work with him. On his job sites, I learned firsthand the DIY skills necessary to do minor home improvement projects such as painting, lighting, carpentry and more, plus the amount of time it took to get it done. In college, interior decorating wasn't on my radar yet. Although I enjoyed the dramatic arts, I still heard my abuela's voice advising me on job security, so I decided to pursue a degree in broadcast journalism. I liked the idea of working as a television host focusing on entertainment news; I felt it was an equally creative field communicating in front of a camera. Upon graduation, I mainly worked freelancing for various local television stations. At one point, I moved to Los Angeles to pursue hosting and acting full-time, but I decided to return to Miami after one year when my savings was depleted. I would've regretted more the "what if" had I not taken a leap of faith.

It was all meant to be. When I moved back from Los Angeles, I took a part-time job in retail as an associate in the home section of a catalogue store at the mall. Little by little I started to create the displays in the department by grouping furniture and accessories, and I loved it! It was a form of artistic expression and sparked the same feelings I felt as a teenager when I decorated my bedroom. Eventually, I became the visual merchandiser for the entire store and was responsible for the holiday décor and displays in the store-front windows. Crazy right? Such a full circle moment for me.

I began to love something just as much—if not more—than being in the entertainment business. By this time I noticed the rise of lifestyle programming on television, with design and cooking shows on cable networks becoming extremely popular. Through reality TV, programs were having a direct impact on the lives of homeowners and inspiring viewers. I knew I could do the same! I could use the power of television for a greater good than just entertainment. This gave me a purpose and changed my career path.

All of my experiences in so many areas of my life were converging into one: my keen eye for design that I sharpened as a visual merchandiser; the DIY skills that I learned from my father while working with him on the weekends as a kid; and, of course, my broadcasting background as on-air talent and a producer. I discovered a new passion, and I was determined to combine both of my worlds—my love for design and hosting—on television projects that would help others in the process. I've always believed in the power of visualization to make things a reality. When you see it in your mind, you're putting it out in the Universe, and you will achieve it. The signals were all there that this is what I was meant to do in my life and I saw it clearly. I didn't know how or when it would happen, but I knew it would.

The opportunity came in 2004 when my agent sent me to interview for a general assignment reporter position at a local Miami news station, WSVN—the FOX affiliate. I was hesitant to go at first because I knew I didn't want to cover news, but I saw it as an opportunity to pitch the idea of a home décor segment to the news director. And as they say, the rest is history. For twelve years I was the host and designer of a segment called "Room for Improvement." It was the first of its kind on local news, and the concept was to decorate a room in one day, while sharing design tips with viewers on how to work with what they already had to give their home a decorator look for less.

During this time I became known as the Makeover Maestro, transforming interior and exterior spaces by doing everything to turn my vision for a room into a reality: painting, electrical and shopping—to make it all happen in one day! I came up with the concept of one-day makeovers to inspire homeowners to do the same by not making the process so daunting. To this day, home makeover shows on major networks might take two days or more—even weeks or months if remodeling is involved—to complete a transformation, and they have an entire crew assisting behind the scenes. I felt this was not realistic for every homeowner watching, so I made a conscious decision to set my work apart by focusing on one-day makeovers that were just as impressive. And when I say one day, I'm not referring to having 24 hours to transform a room; it really meant I had about eight hours, which is a standard work schedule. When the demand for my services began to increase, I launched my own home-styling business that specializes in one-day makeovers, called The WOW Factor!, Inc.

Currently, I'm blessed to be the host and design expert on a weekly program that airs in South Florida on the ABC affiliate, WPLG. The show is called So Flo Home Project, and I continue to do what I love—changing lives one room at a time. I've been given an amazing platform for the last three years as the host of ION@Home for ION Television network, and I also contribute design segments to Telemundo's national Spanish-language morning program, Un Nuevo Día. It's a lot, but I'm grateful for it all. Even on days when I get tired, I take a moment to realize this is the life I dreamed about and that I worked hard to create.

My biggest life lesson has been to be who you are, love what you do and everything else will fall in its place. The person I feared disappointing the most, my abuela, was my biggest supporter and would call our family and friends to watch me whenever I was on television or appeared in a magazine. I know she was proud of me, and she accepted me for who I was. Through it all I've learned my path happened exactly how it needed to happen, and I'm exactly where I need to be right now. I've learned to trust in the timing of things and where the Universe takes you. The fact that you're reading this book now is not a coincidence.

CHAPTER 1

Three Steps to Decorating Any Room for Less

Learn the Design Principles That Will Help You Turn Your House into Your Dream Home

Let me introduce you to my concept of the three steps to decorating a room: walls, furniture and accessories. I decided to break down the design process into three parts so that homeowners can learn to approach every decorating project in the same manner I do—just like a professional designer. In my opinion, you cannot have a finished "decorator room" unless all three steps are in place. It's my job as a designer to point out changes that can have a big impact in the look and feel of your home. Above all, I think there's a misconception that decorating is a long and tedious process, but by following these steps and doing the necessary prep work like shopping ahead of time, the actual transformation of a room can happen in one day—if you're up to the challenge!

So how do we achieve a one-day makeover? Let me clarify by saying that it doesn't happen spontaneously on the same day you decide to redecorate. I wish I could blink my eyes like a genie to make it that easy. It does require planning, and you have to do your homework like painting the walls or shopping for the new furniture and accessories that you will need to update the room. The goal is to have all the décor elements accessible in your home, like pieces to complete a puzzle. This is the same process I follow when I work on any room makeover on and off television. I make sure I have all the tools and materials, furniture and accessories with me to achieve a dramatic before and after in one day.

No two rooms are the same, so this will affect the amount of time and money you need to invest when shopping for the makeover. Some spaces might require a redesign, which means you're working with elements already in the home; by adding new minimal accent furniture and accessories you're able to refresh the look. In other situations, you might be starting over with a completely empty room. These are two realistic scenarios, and in both cases, you have to shop beforehand and prepare the room for the makeover to take place. This can also include hiring a licensed and insured painter, electrician or handyman—if you don't consider yourself to be a do-it-yourself enthusiast in these areas.

That being said, I purposely did not include a chapter on kitchen and bathroom spaces in the book because the reality is it will take more than one day to achieve a complete room makeover. I rarely get a chance to work on them on my television show for this reason. I grappled with this decision. Yes, there are minor cosmetic fixes you can consider, such as a new tile backsplash or vanity or new appliances that will help you update these rooms, but the timeline will require a weekend or more, and more than likely you will have to contract other service providers that specialize in remodeling and construction to achieve a full room makeover—especially when dealing with countertops, flooring, cabinets and plumbing. These are projects that fall outside the scope of decorating.

Staying true to the concept of the book, the three steps to decorating a room are guidelines that will help you save money and avoid costly mistakes throughout the entire process, from shopping to decorating, so the end result is a beautiful room you feel proud of because you were inspired to think like a designer. Whether it's the excitement of decorating a first home, but not knowing where to start, or you're looking for ways to refresh your current style, it doesn't matter if you own or rent, live in a single-family dwelling or an apartment. You deserve to create the home of your dreams. Are you ready?

1 Walls

As a design expert, I understand the decorating process can be overwhelming. You might realize you need help, but you don't know where to begin—especially when you start with an empty room as a blank canvas, where the options are limitless.

Decorating a room is done in layers. And when all the layers are in place you end up with a finished room. Therefore, the first step addresses the walls because they play an important role as the backdrop to your design concept. I know what you're thinking: how do I come up with a design concept and what color? How do I choose a color? We've all been there and it happens to me, too, with every makeover. Color is an important design element used to set a mood or make a statement. It can energize a room or have a calming effect, which means it can evoke an emotional response in us, both mentally and physically. What I suggest is that you find an inspiration piece as your jumping-off point. This will give you a general idea of the color scheme and style you like as a way to keep you focused and, by doing so, the end result will be a cohesive design just like a professional. An inspiration piece can come from artwork, a piece of fabric or even a place you've visited.

Inspiration Board

To narrow down a particular style, gather design ideas in a folder and fill it with photos of rooms that caught your attention from magazines, catalogues, decorating blogs and furniture stores. Find common elements that you love and use that as your inspiration, so it is reflected in the design concept of your room. You can even create a vision board with clippings of your favorite furniture pieces, fabric swatches, color samples and any other details. This becomes your wish list to make it a reality. Don't be too concerned if you can't afford to buy the exact pieces; this is about being inspired to create a similar look in your home within your budget—not recreate the room in the photo.

Color Theories

The inspiration piece or photo taken from a magazine can be a resource for choosing a color scheme for the room. I've been doing this for so long that I have the ability to choose a wall color that works based on existing furnishings and flooring. It's safe to say the most popular color in design right now is gray. It's considered the new beige in home décor. It's a neutral hue that works in every room and in every shade, but this doesn't mean it's the right color for you just because it's on trend.

Regardless of what base color you start with, I want to go over the basics of a color wheel, so you have the professional knowledge to create harmonious and beautiful color combinations in any room. This information applies to choosing paint and decorating, so it's a good foundation as you begin to work on your design plan.

Consider this a refresher course in art class. The color wheel is designed so that virtually any colors you pick from it will look good together. It is divided into three primary colors: red, yellow and blue; three secondary colors: green, orange and purple, which are created by mixing two primary colors; and then another six tertiary colors, which are created by mixing primary and secondary colors.

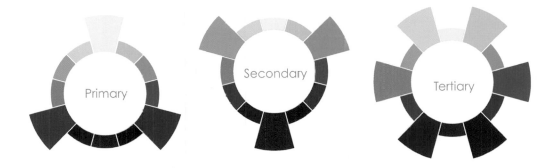

The color wheel can also be separated in half into warm and cool colors. Warm colors are energetic and vibrant (red, yellow, orange) and command attention in a room. Warm colors are good choices for large rooms because they visually bring in the walls, making the space feel more intimate. Cool colors, on the other hand, are calm and soothing (blue, green, purple) and create the illusion that the walls recede, making a small room appear spacious. These are terms used in interior design, so it helps to have a visual when we reference warm and cool colors. White, black and gray are considered to be neutral because they are void of color. This is the reason they complement any color palette.

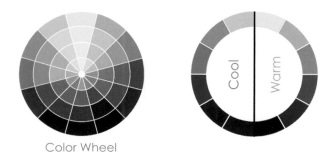

Color Wheel

Are you with me so far? In addition to warm and cool colors, there are three things that can affect the intensity of the hue (aka, color): tint, tone and shade. Tint refers to the mixture of a pure hue with white, which makes it lighter and more subdued; tone is the result when a pure hue is mixed with gray (black and white), which makes the color "toned-down" or less saturated; and shade is the mixture of a pure hue with black, which makes it more intense and darker. Although homeowners use these terms interchangeably when referencing color, they all have different meanings. These terms are important because you can control the depth and contrast of a room simply by knowing there are different values of the same color, from lightest to darkest.

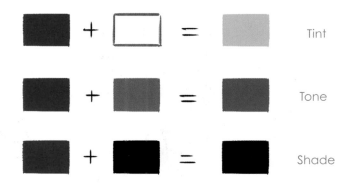

How would you apply this to your home? This is most helpful when you consider the natural light coming into the room. Lighter colors (tinted) reflect more light than darker (shaded), so if your room has few windows and you wish to make it brighter, choose light-reflecting colors that are cool. On the opposite spectrum, if your room is already too bright due to direct sunlight, a darker shade will prevent the color from looking washed out.

Color Schemes

Once you decide on a color that you like on the wheel or in your inspiration piece, you can select different combinations to balance and add depth in a room. The most popular color schemes are listed below, which are a good starting point to play with your color story.

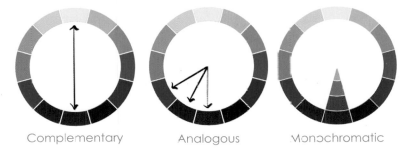

Complementary   Analogous   Monochromatic

Complementary Scheme is the simplest because it uses two colors that sit opposite each other on the color wheel. This combination is bold due to the extremely high contrast, so it's best if one color acts as the dominant shade and the other as an accent, and combine with neutrals to tone down the intensity.

Analogous Color Scheme is when you use three colors adjacent to each other on the color wheel. For this to be successful there's actually a decorating formula called the 60–30–10 Rule as a guideline, which is used to balance the proportion of colors in a room. This means 60 percent will be the dominant color, 30 percent will be a secondary color, while 10 percent is an accent color.

Monochromatic Color Scheme uses variations in lightness and saturation of a single color. Monochromatic colors are clean and elegant, and go well together, producing a soothing effect. You can create a similar color scheme using neutrals, which is one of my personal favorites. Simply choose black, white and gray in lieu of brighter shades.

I know this is a lot to digest, but the reason I wanted to include this information is so you have a basic understanding of color theories when you're coming up with a color palette for a room, which usually begins with paint. The color wheel acts like a blueprint to assist you in the other decorating steps as well when you begin to select furniture and accessories. Most importantly, when it comes to paint remember that it is not permanent and you can always change it. Rules are certainly meant to be broken as you come up with your own individual style.

Paint Samples

Once you've determined a color palette, take into consideration the size of the space and how much or little natural light it receives. Light in any form, whether it's natural or artificial, and even the direction your room faces will have an effect on the appearance of the color.

As the day progresses from sunrise to noon, late afternoon and dusk, the light changes in intensity, and the color will look different from the paint chip. A room with east exposure will appear brighter in the morning as the sun rises and can benefit from warm colors; the opposite will happen in a room with west exposure. In the morning, the light is dull, so cool colors will complement the space. In north-facing rooms, the sunlight is less direct and cooler throughout most of the day, so you can add warm colors to balance the light; and in south-facing rooms, colors are intensified, so cool hues soften the light it receives throughout the day. These are merely guidelines to help you with your color selection. You can adjust the intensity of the hue to make a specific warm or cool color work with the direction your room faces. Another factor to consider is how much time you'll be spending in the room during the morning or night.

This is why it's so important to buy samples of your top two or three colors and test them first on your wall. Observe them during all light changes, because you want to make sure you're happy with the selection before you paint all the walls.

The next decision you have to make is the sheen. Paint comes in everything from flat to high gloss, and selecting the right sheen depends on the application: walls, trims or doors. Without getting overly complicated, the rule of thumb is the higher the sheen, the more durable and washable the paint is; however, it will also draw attention to any imperfections because it reflects more light. Therefore, I don't recommend a satin or semi-gloss sheen on textured walls, but it is ideal on trim. My personal preference is to use matte or eggshell finish on the walls, and satin on the interior trim. It will still give you a durable and beautiful finish. Trim refers to all millwork that make up the architectural details of a room installed around walls, floors and ceilings. This includes baseboards, door and window casings, crown moldings and railings, to name a few. Buy the paint already premixed with the primer to save you time and especially if you're going from a darker color to a lighter one. Every paint brand has brochures on this subject matter at home improvement and specialty paint stores. I know painting is not for everyone, but it is one of the easiest ways to save money by doing it yourself and not hiring a professional.

Paint samples of your favorite colors and label them to determine how they will look in your room. Remember that a color swatch can look very different on the walls.

Accent Walls

I've walked into many homes where an accent wall is highlighted in a room. The intent is to create a focal point by painting one wall in a completely different color. This can also be done with different materials such as wallpaper or molding or artwork, but often times it's achieved with paint because it's a quick and inexpensive way to give a space a makeover without necessarily painting all the walls. Often times the wrong wall or color was chosen and it throws off the visual balance of the room.

Generally speaking, an accent wall is the first wall that catches your eye when you walk into a room. It can have a fireplace, media center or be the most expansive wall behind a sofa, bed or dining table. This is the feature wall you wish to turn into a design statement. In an open floor plan, it also helps to create a visual separation of spaces. You can be as bold or subtle as you want; the only guideline for an accent wall to be effective is that it should be painted the darkest or most vivid color in the room compared to the adjacent walls. Look for colors on the outer edges of the color wheel that have the most saturation. If you like neutral palettes, simply choose darker shades of the existing wall color; or add a splash with a complementary or analogous color scheme as long as you tie the color in with the accessories throughout the space.

If more than two-thirds of the wall is covered with windows and doors or it's shared by two rooms as part of an open concept, I don't recommend painting it an accent color. There will be minimal impact by trying to make these walls stand out.

Wall Coverings

Design trends today go beyond using paint to transform a blank wall. There are other treatments you can consider to make a statement in a room. They include geometric and textured wallpaper, natural elements like wood and stone, fun chalkboard paint, photographic and landscape murals, and rustic and modern tiles. These materials can definitely add a wow factor, but in most cases the best application is on a feature wall so it doesn't overpower the room. This means instead of covering the entire room with the material, we are creating a focal point on one wall. In subsequent chapters I include some of these creative finishes in the room makeovers, so you can see the most effective way to use them to complement any design.

2 Furniture

Furniture defines the purpose of the room and transforms it into a functional space. Now that the backdrop is set with your walls, this is the step where you have to consider your lifestyle to make sure the furnishings meet all of your needs—including the family, sometimes even pets. Be realistic about this because even though you might envision white, modern sofas in your home, does it really work with children or pets? Probably not. However, don't be discouraged; you can still create a modern look with a gray sofa and white throw pillows to achieve a similar style. This is where you begin to play with your color palette as you select the furniture.

Think of the different activities you will do in the room and how many people it needs to accommodate. For example, in a living room you might want seating for at least five to watch television and entertain friends. In a dining room, a table for six or eight works best for larger gatherings. There will be numerous options on display at the furniture showroom, so it's important that you refer back to your inspiration board to maintain a cohesive style. It's okay to blend different elements from several decorating styles together through small pieces and accessories, but the main furniture in the room will define the look.

Measure and Outline

As you begin to shop for pieces, I suggest you do a preliminary scouting trip at the furniture stores. This means you're simply looking, so try to resist an impulse buy. Before you make a single purchase, write down measurements of everything that you like. The wrong furniture scale will work against you in creating a beautiful space. I've seen many homeowners make this mistake and get the furniture delivered only to realize it's too big for their room. I know everything looks great in the showroom, but you have to visualize the furniture within the square footage of your own home. The best way to do that is to outline all the furniture pieces on the floor using painter's tape to map out an arrangement based on the measurements you took (see photos below). This will help you double-check that everything will actually fit the way you envision it.

Again, I cannot emphasize how important it is to buy furniture that is the right scale. While you're at it, also measure door openings and be aware of any tight corners to turn or narrow stairwells to make sure the furniture fits once it gets delivered.

Floor Plan

The furniture placement will be guided by your floor plan. The most important question you need to answer is what will be the focal point of the room? Typically, it's the feature wall as you enter and the furniture arrangement takes place around that item. It can be a fireplace, a TV console or even a blank wall you can turn into a focal point with artwork or wallpaper or architectural molding. Play with different layout options and keep in mind not all the furniture needs to be pushed up against the wall. You can create a cozy and comfortable grouping in the center of the room, too.

As you're mapping out your furniture placement be aware of the natural traffic patterns in and out of the room. This will also determine the scale of the furniture that you buy and how it will be arranged in the room. A poor layout can affect the look and function of the space—no matter how big or small. Some layouts might be more straight-forward, like in a dining room, whereas other areas are more flexible. In the chapters where you have more than one option for furniture groupings, I share tips on the proper scale, placement and combinations that work best to maximize your room's floor plan.

Before you purchase any furniture create an outline on the floor with painter's tape to help you visualize if it will fit in the room.

Before

Small-Space Furniture

Luckily, you don't have to sacrifice comfort and style if you're furnishing a small space or live in an apartment. There are a few tricks designers use to make a room appear bigger.

Choose furniture that has clean lines and tight upholstery to improve sight lines and minimize visual clutter. Pay attention to how close a sofa sits on the ground because believe it or not, raised furniture on legs will create the illusion of more space in your floor plan. I know, right? Major furniture brands now offer a line of apartment-size furnishings, which are specifically tailored for small spaces by occupying a reduced footprint. For example, a standard sofa is 84 inches (213.5 cm) wide and a comparable style in an apartment size is between 68 and 72 inches (162.5 and 183.0 cm) in width. It's similar to buying clothes in petite sizes to fit your body; there's a perfect "style size" solution for every room.

Other details to look for are open-style bottoms on tables and glass tops, which don't appear heavy in a room. Often times, room décor is limited to the square footage on the floor, but take advantage of vertical space by mixing in some taller pieces, like a bookcase or open shelving. Multifunctional furniture is another way to avoid overcrowding. Items like a bed that includes storage underneath, coffee table with drawers, and stools that can be used as side tables and seating are great design features that maximize a small space. I promise you can still create a beautiful home that the entire family can enjoy if you look for the furniture that meets your organizational needs and is the right fit.

3 Accessories

The third step is where everything comes together to create a space that is a true reflection of you. Your walls might have a fresh coat of paint, and the furniture will make the room functional, but without the decorative accessories, the style factor will still be missing. Without them, a room looks incomplete—dare I say naked—since the

decorative accessories are the final details that bring the design concept to life During the majority of the consultations with clients, I find this is the step that is mainly missing in their homes, and ironically, it's the least expensive when you compare purchasing a high-ticket item like furniture to a small accent piece like a lamp. This is truly my favorite part of the makeover because I'm dressing the room for the big reveal. As you begin to place every accent in the room you will see it transform right before your eyes!

Decorative accessories are the accents in a room—everything from lighting, window treatments, artwork and throw pillows. These are the touches that give a room personality and help turn a house into a home.

Artwork

Art is very personal. As a homeowner, you should have a connection to the images you see on the walls. This doesn't mean you can't buy generic art in a home store, but you definitely want the piece to have some sort of meaning in your life and tie in with your decorating style. It's also a way to tell your story by seeing beautiful art, prints or even photographs that represent your interests. Otherwise, you're staring at empty walls, which will give the impression that you just recently moved in.

The main issue I find during consultations is homeowners don't know how to properly select the scale in relation to the size of the wall. There's also a misconception that every wall needs to have something on it, which is totally not true. In the design world, negative space is the blank space that surrounds an object and helps to bring balance to a room. In layman's terms, it can simply mean less is more. It's important that you don't visually overcrowd each wall with stuff to the point that you can't take a moment to appreciate any of it.

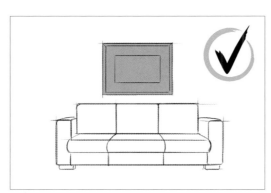

How to Hang Artwork at the Correct Height

Hanging artwork in a room can also be tricky for many homeowners. If you hang it too high, there's a complete disconnect in the room between the frame and the décor. A "rule" that has been around for a while is to hang the center of the artwork at eye level. However, this doesn't make sense to me because the height of the person can vary. We're all different! Ceiling height also has to be taken into account.

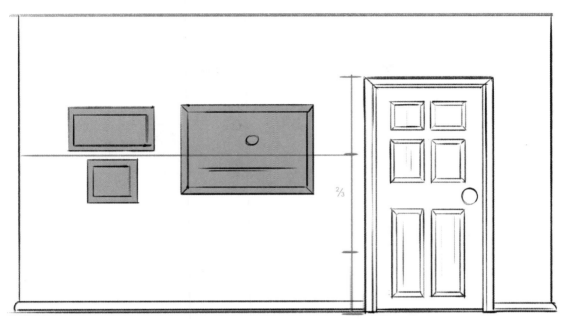

Maintain a consistent sight level throughout a room by hanging artwork two-thirds up the length of the door.

My personal preference is to use a window or door frame as a better reference to hang the artwork. These architectural details are important elements in residential design, and the headers are usually installed at the same height throughout a room for visual consistency. Generally speaking, the center of the artwork should hang two-thirds up from the bottom of the door or window. This determines "eye level" based on the room's actual height and not the person, which to me is a more accurate way to achieve an arrangement that is in harmony with the room. I tested this method throughout my own home and the measurement was pretty spot-on—give or take a couple of inches.

Lighting

In design, there are three main types of lighting used in a room: ambient, task and accent. Ambient lighting refers to the general illumination of the environment. The main ceiling fixture in a room would be considered ambient lighting as an artificial light source at night, but during the day, a window can certainly be a natural source of ambient lighting in a room. Task lighting is used to illuminate a small, specific area like a desk lamp, which allows more light while you're working or a floor lamp next to a sofa for reading; and finally there is accent lighting, which is used to highlight certain areas of an interior space. This includes lamps on side tables or picture lights over artwork. They shine a spotlight and focus your attention to an item or area.

It's good to familiarize yourself with these different types of lighting because every room should have a balance of the three to ensure interior spaces are properly lit for functionality, mood and atmosphere. There are many sources of light, such as pendants, sconces, table or floor lamps, and the style you choose will have a direct impact on the look of the room.

Bulb & Wattage

The type of bulb and wattage also has a direct effect on how the colors and space is perceived. Color temperature is a description of the warmth or coolness of a light source, and there are three primary types for incandescent light bulbs: soft white, which are best for bedrooms, living rooms and dining rooms because they give off a warm and cozy feel; bright white/cool white are great for kitchens, bathrooms or garages because it's whiter and gives the room more energy; and finally daylight is also a good option for bathrooms, kitchens and basements. It provides the greatest contrast among colors and is effective for working on projects or applying makeup. Technology has advanced to include CFL (compact fluorescents) and LED (light-emitting diode), which last longer, are more energy-efficient and can also be purchased in different color temperatures.

In most cases, the higher the ceiling, the higher the wattage should be because it has more area to light up, and vice versa. This will depend on the size of the room and how you wish for it to function. For example, in a more intimate setting like a dining room, higher wattage might not be essential—especially when you're balancing the light between other sources such as a chandelier, sconces and recessed lighting.

Every space will have a different set of needs, but be mindful of hiring an electrician when dealing with fixtures that require hardwiring such as a chandelier, or installing a dimmer switch, which allows you to control the brightness of the lighting in a room. Another feature you can look for when shopping for lamps is a three-way setting. It's clearly written on the socket and allows you to control the brightness of the light by simply turning the knob switch.

Window Treatments

From lighting we move on to window treatments. Although blinds and verticals are functional because they control the light coming into a room and add privacy, I don't necessarily consider them to be decorative unless they are plantation shutters. Curtain panels always add an extra layer of elegance and are also a great opportunity to add color and texture in a room that ties back to your inspirational color palette.

There are many different styles of panels to choose from and each reflects a certain look.

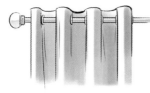
Grommets

Grommets/Rings – The rings can be found already inserted in the fabric or you can purchase them separately and clip along the top edge. This reflects a more casual and contemporary style, which is very popular. The curtain rod is exposed, which also makes it a design feature. A tip is to match the color of the ring to the rod for a cohesive look. If you need the curtains to be functional, meaning you will be opening and closing them to control the light and/or privacy, these work best because they easily slide across the curtain rod.

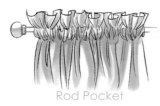
Rod Pocket

Rod-Pocket – The curtain panels slip onto the rod through a pocket found on the top edge. The more panels you place on the rod, the more bunching up or gathering of fabric will happen, which is the desired look with this style. If you use too little, it has the tendency to resemble a flat bed sheet hanging from the window—not very attractive. Although I'm not a huge fan of this traditional style, it can have a place on a small window or nursery space where the panels will be used mainly as décor—meaning stationary—because they are more difficult to open and close. However, you can easily address this by adding curtain rings.

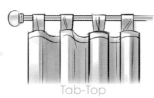
Tab-Top

Tab-Top – This look is more casual and relaxed. It has loops of fabric sewn along the top edge of the panel. This exposes the curtain rod and allows the fabric to hang flat. In my opinion, this type of panel works better in a traditional, country-style or kids room. I tend not to use them as often.

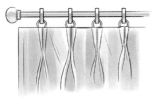

Pleated

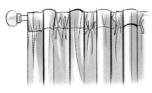

Hidden Tab

Pleated – This style is definitely a lot more formal. The pleating effects on the top edge of the curtains reflect a very elegant and classic look. The fabrics tend to be lined to give it a heavier weight. The pleats create a beautiful fold on the panels that are evenly spaced and can be hung from a rod using rings or hooks on a traverse rod.

Hidden Tab-Top – This is one of my favorite styles! It combines the look of a pleated and grommet panel, but in a much simpler way. The tabs of fabric are hidden behind the top edge. Once the rod is inserted through the loops on the back, it creates a natural fold on the fabric and the rod stays completely disguised behind the panel. It's beautiful and contemporary. It can be casual, yet formal in the right setting without looking too fussy. Love, love, love.

Curtain Width & Length

The number of panels you need is determined by the size of the window. Measure the width of the window or sliding door and double the number to determine the amount of panels. This will give the window a fuller look on either side when the panels are open and still provide enough coverage for privacy when closed. Unless you buy custom-made window treatments, more than likely you will not be able to achieve the coverage and fullness you need with only one panel on each side. This is the reason that when you buy window treatments in home stores, you might need four (two panels on each side) or six (three panels on each side) to get the look you need. As long as you buy the correct amount of panels, the seam between them won't be noticeable when you close them. When they are pulled back to the sides, it's not an issue at all. I find this is a fair compromise for the savings of not going the custom route.

Also, don't be limited by the structural height or width of the window itself. To create the illusion of a taller room, install the curtain rod close to the ceiling and extend past the width of the window by 6 to 12 inches (15 to 30.5 cm) on either side. This will make the room brighter since the window won't be partially blocked by fabric once the curtains are open during the day. This is a visual trick designers use to draw your eye upwards and make the window more prominent on the wall as an architectural feature of the room. Installing the curtain rod higher and wider than the window frame will affect the measurements for the length and amount of panels that you need, so keep this in mind.

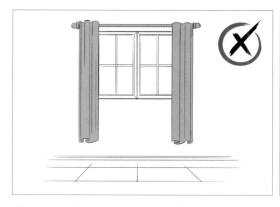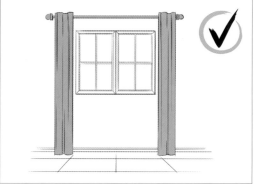

Floor-length curtain panels are ideal in any room for a designer look.

Standard curtain lengths that you can purchase directly off the shelf in department stores include 84 (213.5 cm), 96 (244 cm) and 108 inches (274.5 cm). Typically, anything longer falls into the special or custom order category, which can be more expensive. A mistake I often encounter in homes is when the panels are installed too high from the floor. I compare this to wearing pants with a hem that is too short—it always looks strange. They can look as if they were installed by an amateur. In all my designs and for a professional-looking install, all curtain panels should brush up against the floor or about 1 to 2 inches (2.5 to 5 cm) of the hem should rest on it for a softer look. It adds more drama and height in any room.

Area Rugs

An inspiration for your color palette can certainly come from an area rug. They add warmth in a room over hardwood floors or tiles and visually ground the furniture grouping—especially in an open-concept home, which is a desired floor plan by homeowners. When one space flows into another and there is no structural separation, like a wall, for example, rugs are key design elements to define an area.

They are also a great accessory that can add style and color in a room, yet can be easily removed to change up the look if you get bored since there is no commitment like wall-to-wall carpeting. Buying the proper area rug size is crucial to balancing a room, though. I'll go into that in more depth in each chapter where appropriate, like in living room, dining room or bedroom, but when in doubt, it's best to go larger than smaller. The pattern has to complement and not compete with any other printed fabrics in a room such as throw pillows and curtain panels, so you have to be conscious of mixing large and small patterns, texture and solids to create a visually pleasing look in the room. I'll show you examples of this in the Living Rooms chapter (page 59).

Throw Pillows

Ahh, throw pillows—also referred to as decorative or accent pillows. I can't live without them. They immediately transform a piece of furniture and take it from simple to stylish. They are a decorator tool used to add a pop of color, contrast and texture on a sofa or bed and can make a statement in the room. Throw pillows add balance and can tie an entire color scheme together by pulling colors from artwork or an area rug or an inspiration piece; they add an elegant and polished look and can refresh tired furniture without spending too much money. They come in a wide range of textiles, shapes and sizes, and they are most effective when layered in contrasting fabrics and colors to give the space lots of visual interest. By simply switching out the covers, you can update the look for seasonal décor as well.

Combining throw pillows is similar to putting together an outfit. You have to make sure nothing clashes. Choose pillows that directly relate back to your color palette to maintain a cohesive style. It's best to keep things orderly by keeping the arrangement symmetrical on a sofa or bed—meaning what you do to one side, repeat on the other. Vary the size of the prints between large and small, and break up the pattern with a solid in between. Take into consideration the pattern on the bedding or sofa fabric when combining pillows in such a manner. In addition to solids, plaids and striped pillows also work as a neutral against a busy pattern. Finally, don't go overboard and make sure the size of the pillow is proportional to the furniture. In other words, you don't want the pillow to swallow up the furniture or, on the flip side, be too small. The most common throw pillow designs are square and range from 16 to 24 inches (40.5 to 61 cm). On average, a 20-inch (51-cm) size works well on most furniture.

Décor Accents

I've highlighted the general categories of accessories that fall within this third decorating step; however, the smaller accents, which can be more personal, are what give a room their finishing touch. This includes candles, books, photo frames, plants, decorative trays and more. How you "accessorize" a room with these items can make a world of difference. The challenging part for many homeowners is how to group them in an attractive manner on a table or shelf. In the Living Rooms chapter (page 64) I discuss this more in depth, but the general guideline is to create groupings of these smaller items and vary the heights of the collection for visual interest.

The goal is to create mini focal points within a larger table surface that complement the room setting and don't create clutter—not too much, but just enough. One such form of these accents is candleholders that work in every room setting. I'm a big fan of using them as accent lighting and for the cozy ambience they create. I know it can be a safety issue if you have small children or even pets running around the house, so a good alternative is to use flameless, battery-operated candles. These give you the same look, without the risk.

Throughout the book pay close attention to the different groupings I create in the various room settings. It will demonstrate how to effectively incorporate these accents in your décor as the final "jewelry" to complete the look. These small accents will be unique to you.

Decorating Budget

At this point, the last question you need to ask yourself is what is your budget? Like any designer, you need to know how much money you have to work with to shop for any new items on your wish list. Keep in mind the biggest expense will always be new furniture, and it takes a good chunk of any budget from the get-go. Don't get discouraged when you think of everything you want to do in the entire home because what I really want you to do is focus on one room at a time. This is how I built my business doing one-day makeovers, indeed, by focusing only on one room. The decorating process doesn't get overwhelming and you're able to control costs this way.

Based on experience, I inform new clients that $1,000 can be easily spent on items considered to be decorative accessories: the rugs, lamps, artwork and so on. If new furniture is required I would add an additional $1,000 to $2,000. It can be higher, but it depends on the size of the room and how much furniture needs to be purchased. This does not include fees for additional contractors and/or labor to tackle areas you might not feel comfortable doing yourself, like painting, electrical or carpentry. The budget I'm referencing is also based on merchandise you can buy at local furniture retailers and discount home décor stores, which is where I do the bulk of my shopping. Just to be clear, this means no high-end specialty shops or custom-made furnishings; however, I know with the ideas in this book you can still achieve the decorator look for less since a frugal budget forces you to be the most creative, which is why I love what I do! There are so many places you can shop for home décor to save money, including big-box retailers and online catalogues, from furniture and discounted home stores to garage sales and antique markets. The "hunt" becomes part of the fun to snatch the best bargain.

DIY Design

The easiest way to stretch your decorating dollar is to take on a do-it-yourself project in every room. This is why I illustrate a design idea in each chapter that everyone can do at home as it relates to a given space. Whether it's how to build your own headboard in a bedroom out of doors or personalize furniture to give it a unique style, it's a step-by-step guide that you can follow to not only save money, but also make something special that can't be store bought. I know home improvement stores can be intimidating and you only venture inside if you need to buy paint or light bulbs, but I use it as a great resource to shop for basic materials that I can creatively transform in my makeovers. I promise you no major carpentry skills are required since in most cases the store can even cut the wood to the size that you need. Did you know that? I enjoy walking up and down the aisles exploring their inventory to see what project ideas I can come up with that will give me a lot of impact for less.

Lumber Sizes and Measurements

Lumber is cut to a specific length, width and depth. If you're considering purchasing wood for any of the projects I highlight in this book, and, of course, I urge you to do so, it's important to know that there is a difference between the nominal size (the label put on the lumber you buy) and the actual size. The nominal measurements are when the board is first rough sawn from the log, but the actual measurements are smaller after the board is dried and planed smooth on all four sides in the milling process. Example, a 2 x 4-inch (5 x 10-cm) lumber is actually reduced to a finished size of 1½ x 3½ inches (4 x 9 cm). As you take measurements to build a project, keep this in mind.

Home improvement stores are a great place to shop for decorative items including table lamps, window treatments, area rugs, shelving, mirrors and even furniture online. Typically, it's the last place a homeowner might think about to go shopping to decorate their home, but I'm here to tell you they sell so much more than remodeling and construction supplies.

The goal with the DIY projects is to inspire you to see common construction supplies as a great tool for creating something you can feel proud of displaying in your home. It's another affordable option to decorate your home with one-of-a-kind accent pieces that no one else owns. What matters is not the actual cost of the item, but how you put it all together in the room that will make it look more expensive. It's like original art!

Three Steps to Decorating a Room

By breaking down the decorating process into three basic steps—walls, furniture and accessories—you see first-hand how each layer builds off each other to give a room a makeover. These are the same steps I use for every design project I work on, and I love sharing them with you so that you can become your own designer as you decorate your home.

Take a moment to look around each room in your home and see what steps you feel are missing. You might already have nice furniture, but you could be missing the decorative accessories; maybe a new paint color is required to make it all come together nicely for you; or maybe it's a combination of all of the above, but at least you know how to start and what to look for to create a room that makes you happy. Every room will pose a different set of challenges and needs, but the decorating steps remain the same. Just remember to reference the inspiration board as you are coming up with a design concept to ensure that the execution of your vision will be successful. I know you can do it!

Design Your Life

When you complete a room, I want you to take a step back and take it all in. As I've mentioned before, decorating goes beyond the physical look of the room. To me, it's equally important to think of ways you can interact with the space as a way of feeding your spirit. I know you're probably confused right now, but what I mean by this is simply creating a moment that will allow you to experience your new space on a different level as a way to appreciate your surroundings more.

This can be done by creating a cozy corner in your bedroom to sit and read a book—instead of only using the bedroom for sleeping; or lighting a candle when you sit around your dinner table—even though there is no special occasion to celebrate. Moments like these bring simple joys and embrace a lifestyle you might otherwise be too busy to think about. They serve as a gentle reminder to stop and be present, enjoying the beautiful home you have created for yourself. You designed the room you wanted; now you can design the life you wish to live in it.

Before

DIY Design
Painted Accent Wall

Do you have a nice headboard, but still feel your bedroom is too simple? You can create a more dramatic backdrop behind the bed by painting it a darker color than the rest of the walls. It's easy, and it's something we can do together.

Color and pattern can make a world of difference in any room, and one way to achieve this is with paint. Luckily, it's also the easiest and most inexpensive way to transform a room. Many homeowners have never picked up a brush or roller and would rather hire a professional painter to take on the job for fear of doing something incorrect. Well, it's actually easier than drawing in a coloring book because you don't have to stay within the lines. The wall becomes one, large blank page and the only areas you need to avoid might be ceiling and baseboards—and to assist us, we have tools of the trade. Prepping the room will ensure the finish is successful, like spackling any holes, covering floors with drop cloths, and protecting trim molding with painter's tape.

I urge you to try it by beginning small and painting a feature or accent wall in your home. It can create a beautiful focal point in a dining room, living room, bedroom or anywhere that you wish to make a statement. By taking on this DIY project you can also save a lot of money you can put toward furnishings and accessories. It can be a substantial savings! Some people even find painting therapeutic. Me, not so much, but I know it's a necessary and an invaluable process of decorating a room, which I can appreciate having worked with my dad when I was a kid.

If it helps, practice on a piece of plywood until you get the hang of it or throw a painting party with friends who can all pitch in and help. I promise you can do this and you'll be proud of yourself when it's completed. In fact, you might find the urge to continue painting other rooms in your home.

Materials

Paint

Drop cloths

Lightweight spackling paste and putty knife

Sanding block

Painter's tape

Ladder

2″ (5-cm) trim brush (angled tip)

Touch-up and trim tray

Paint tray

Roller cover with frame

Extension pole

Steps

1. The first step is determining how much paint you need. Most accent walls only require 1 gallon (38 L) of paint, which covers on average 350 square feet (106 m²) with one coat. If you wish to buy paint for an entire room, add the length of all the walls and multiply by the room height from floor to ceiling in feet to get the square footage of the room. Then divide this number by 350 square feet (106 m²). This calculation includes the surface for doors and windows, which are either not paintable or might be painted in a different color; however, it's best to have more paint than less; you can save it for future touch-ups. Always count on giving a wall two coats—even if it has a primer added to the mix. Paint with primer costs more, but it's still worth it because it saves you time and steps.

2. Cover your floors with drop cloths along the edge of your baseboard and remove any outlet wall plates. If necessary, use a damp cloth to make sure your walls are clean and free of dust. Fill in any nail holes or cracks with the spackling paste and putty knife. Feather the edges to ensure a smooth finish. Allow 30 minutes to dry or follow recommended set time. Sometimes a light sanding is required using a fine sanding block to smooth the surface where spackling paste was applied.

3. Apply painter's tape all around the perimeter of the wall, ceiling and baseboard to protect surfaces that are not going to be painted and use a ladder for those areas hard to reach. Make sure you press down on the edge to seal it or paint will seep underneath. If your walls and ceilings are textured, the tape won't stick easily, so it's better to mask with a straightedge such as a ruler or drywall knife. Angle it slightly, and continuously wipe off the paint from the straightedge when you reach a natural stopping point.

4. Dip the edge of the trim brush less than halfway up the bristles and remove excess on the edge of the touch-up and trim tray. The paint should not be dripping at all from brush. Novice DIYers make the mistake of submersing the entire brush. Cut in all the edges first near the painter's tape where the roller cannot reach. Do a series of short strokes working in three-foot sections to maintain a wet edge, overlapping where you left off. If you find there are areas that need more coverage, it's best to wait until it dries for a second coat.

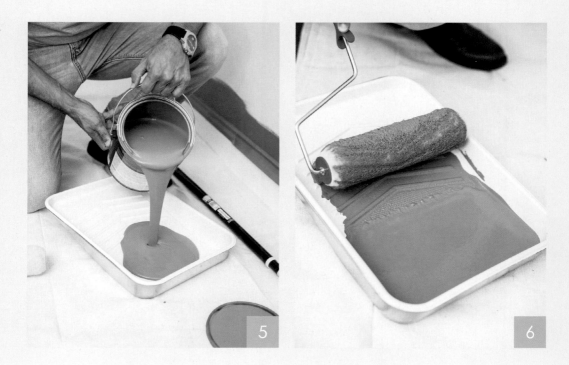

5. Pour paint into the bottom edge of the paint tray and insert your roller into the roller frame. There are rollers for different wall textures and sizes that refer to the depth of the nap pile: very smooth, for metal doors and plaster; smooth and semi-smooth, for drywall; semi-rough, for rough wood and acoustic tile; rough, for textured ceilings and stucco finishes; and very rough, for concrete block, brick and fences. I don't want to confuse you, but generally speaking, the longer the nap, the more paint it will hold. Most homes have smooth to light-textured walls, so you can use a ⅜-inch (1-cm) nap to paint these surfaces. Refer to the packaging on the roller cover and match to your wall texture.

6. Dip roller into the paint and cover all the surfaces by pressing against the ribbed portion of the tray in between rotations. This also removes excess paint.

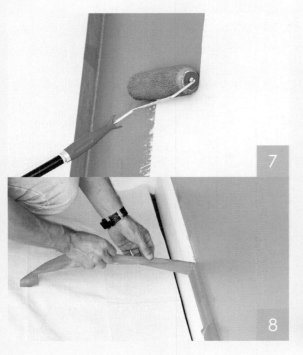

7. Begin by rolling the paint on the wall in one direction, overlapping where you cut in with the brush around the edges. I've heard of forming a w shape as you paint small 3 x 3-inch (7.5 x 7.5-cm) sections, but I'm not a fan of this. I prefer long sections from ceiling to floor using an extension pole, forming columns and overlapping each one as you move across the wall. Let the paint dry for about 30 minutes to 1 hour and repeat with a second coat if necessary. If you find the edges also need a touch-up, repeat the cut-in steps with the trim brush.

8. Before the paint is fully dry, remove the painter's tape. If you wait too long, you risk peeling the paint where it meets the tape edge.

That's it! Your Painting 101 lesson is now complete.

After

The wall is now a design feature in the bedroom, drawing your attention from the moment you walk in. In about one hour and with less than $60 in materials, we have a stunning look.

LIVE
LAUGH
LOVE

Before

CHAPTER 2

Living Rooms
The Perfect Balance Between Comfort and Style That Welcomes You Home

First impressions are made from the moment someone walks through your front door. Yes, curb appeal can set an expectation from the outside, but how you really live is reflected in the interior of your home. You can portray an exterior that is picture-perfect to your neighbors with a beautifully manicured lawn and flower beds, but there is no hiding the "real" you once you step inside.

If you look around your living room right now, does it reflect your style? Would someone be able to imagine you living there in the same manner that your wardrobe or the scent of your perfume/cologne is associated with your persona? As a designer, I can immediately get an idea of the person living there by the look of their living room. I can also tell immediately what the decorating issues are. It's typically the first room you see as soon as you enter the home, and it sets the tone for the décor in the other spaces. This area is ground zero for the home environment you wish to create for yourself and your family. This is why, whether you recently purchased a new home or are looking to update your current one, my suggestion is to always begin with this space. With the exception of a foyer that is mainly considered a transitional area, a living room is precisely used for what its name implies: living. It welcomes you home every day and showcases your life and style through the furnishings and accessories you chose to tell your visual story. Now is the time to explore how you can combine both style and function to make the décor an extension of who you are and represent the real you.

1 Walls

Similar to an art gallery, the walls in your living room are considered the backdrop where your life is on display and where you get to feature your best design work. The only difference is galleries have white walls on purpose, so the art becomes the focal point. In your case, the walls and everything else in the room become part of the scene that is captured within a frame, so it makes sense to use color to make it come alive. It helps to look at any space in your home as a canvas you are about to paint. The first brush strokes, literally and figuratively, begin by focusing on the walls to create your own masterpiece.

The paint wasn't necessarily the issue in this living room. It had classic gray walls, which worked well with any design style—from traditional to modern. I liked the contrast between the wall color and white baseboard and crown molding. Gray is a neutral that works well with any color scheme, so the main objective with this makeover was to make the wall a focal point that reflected both his and her style. The wife loved the look of rustic wood and whimsical décor, while the husband gravitated more toward a modern style.

For this makeover, a new "paint color" came in the form of stain with the addition of a wood plank wall. It's a modern, yet rustic design statement that was the happy medium for the couple. It became the artwork in the room without the necessity to hang anything else over the wall. There are different ways to achieve this look, such as using reclaimed wood pallets, flooring material or new wood that you can stain and distress as well. In some cases, if you wish to achieve the same visual effect without using real wood, you can opt for wallpaper or self-adhesive vinyl planks. The latter is less expensive and is as easy as peel-and-stick, which means it's not permanent, so it's a great stylish solution for apartment renters.

Instead of covering the entire wall in the wood planks, I decided to make it a decorative panel behind the sofa only. I didn't want it to overpower the living room since the space already had wood flooring and I also wished to leave wall space for artwork.

2 Furniture

Are you happy with your furniture? Or can it be improved? Most homeowners purchase a living room set where all the pieces are part of the same collection. If this is you, you're not alone. There are ways to refresh the look by combining your existing pieces with new ones to personalize the style to you. This is definitely more budget-friendly than starting with an empty room. It might be an easy fix by eliminating your loveseat and adding two new chairs to work with your sofa or switching your traditional coffee table to a cocktail ottoman. Visualize ways to rearrange the setting and dare to be different.

In this makeover, the furniture and accessories were the biggest decorating dilemmas. The living room didn't have a defined sense of style with the furniture. Did the TV trays as end tables give it away? I understand they are functional for eating while watching television in the living room, but hello? I draw the line when the homeowners used them as side tables next to their sofa. (Jokingly, but 'm not kidding.) The living room was screaming for an intervention!

Based on the furniture alone, the room was also suffering from an identity crisis. There was a clash of styles between the bulky, brown leather sofa and the sleek, white loveseat. There's a fine line between what is considered eclectic décor and what is mismatched. This living room fell into the mismatched category because the couple didn't know how to merge their different styles into a cohesive décor marriage.

I started from scratch with the furniture and found the perfect sectional on clearance for only $500. Most furniture stores have a clearance section, so don't hesitate to scan there first before shopping the showroom. Some of the merchandise in the clearance section includes furniture that has been discontinued, floor samples or customer returns, so there is always a great deal to be found and your decorating dollars can go a long way.

If you are shopping for new furniture at a store, don't feel compelled to buy the entire set as you see it in the showroom either. For example, in a living room setting a traditional grouping includes a sofa, loveseat and chair; although the store might offer you a savings for buying all three pieces, if it's too much furniture for the size of your living room, then you're not doing your home justice. Typically, you realize this once the furniture arrives and by then it might be too late—you're stuck with it. Not only can it be quite expensive, but buying too much furniture or the wrong scale will work against you in creating a beautiful space.

I chose this gray chaise sectional because it combines modern style with plush comfort. The clean lines and tufting on the cushions are design details that make a subtle statement. This specific style is better suited for a more formal setting of a living room and is not to be confused with oversized, reclining sectionals that bring a corner piece, left arm and right arm sections or that wrap around in the shape of a boomerang with a high back. You know which ones I'm talking about, right? I refer to them as a dinosaur in the room! I cringe when I see this in a living room because it has the tendency to not only close off a room, but the look is too casual and really belongs in a family or media room, which is a more relaxed setting. A living room should have a combination of elegance and comfort, and this chaise sectional is perfect for that reason. You can combine it with other accent furniture in the living room for additional seating.

Shop for sleeker modular sectionals for a living room and avoid bulky recliner styles that take up too much space.

If your heart is still set on a sectional, my second favorite that can work well in a living room is a modular style. It allows you to rearrange the pieces into different groupings, so you are not limited to just one configuration. You get a lot more bang for your buck because you can create many looks to update the space in the future.

Furniture Layouts

Many homeowners have been conditioned to believe that a living room is made up of a sofa, love seat and chair. This is okay as long as you mix and match the pieces from different collections, so they don't look like they come from the same set and right off the showroom floor. Still, there are other furniture groupings you can consider that add enough seating and a custom style. It really depends on the size of the room, the traffic flow in and out of the space and how brave you feel to go "out of the box" from a traditional layout. I say go for it!

Keep in mind a furniture arrangement is usually done around the focal point of the room and takes into consideration the traffic flow walking in and out the space. In a living room, the grouping can be arranged around a fireplace or TV wall or built-in bookcases. If your space has blank walls, then you have more creative license. In the inspiration room, the TV wall was the focal point and I also had to take into account the traffic flow walking into the home from the front door. This is the reason the furniture grouping is off to the right side of the room.

The furniture used in the room layouts can all be interchangeable depending on the square footage of your living room. For example, a sofa can be replaced with a love seat to create the same grouping; a chair can be any style; and an ottoman can also be interpreted as a pouf or bench—as long as the pieces are the right scale. This all relates back to measuring the furniture beforehand at the store and creating an outline on the floor to see what works best in your space. I make this point because even though I reference a sofa in the layouts, as an example, this doesn't mean it's a "one size fits all." The layouts are to emphasize different seating combinations you can come up with to create a style all your own.

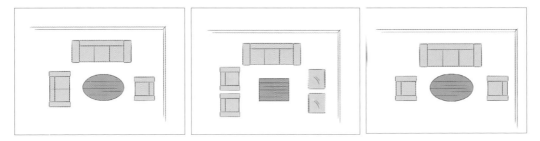

The most popular furniture layouts in a living room include a sofa, love seat, chair and ottoman.

Sofa/Two Chairs

A furniture arrangement consisting of a sofa and two accents chairs is a popular combination. Often times many homeowners use a sofa and loveseat combo. The problem with this is that if your living room is too narrow and part of an open floor plan, the love seat placed at a right angle next to the sofa can block the traffic flow into the rest of the spaces. The solution is to replace the loveseat with two accent chairs instead. The room appears more open and still has enough seating. In the inspiration makeover, I placed the chairs on opposite sides of the room facing each other for two reasons: first, you can engage in a conversation with someone sitting on the sofa and still be able to watch TV; second, the placement doesn't impede the traffic flow into the room from the front door. It's never a good thing if you're bumping into furniture to get from one room to another. In another home setting, placing the accent chairs side by side and across from the sofa can work just fine to balance the arrangement within the room. In design, there are many variables and every home is a different scenario.

Introducing accent chairs in a living room is a perfect opportunity to mix different colors and fabrics on the furniture. For example, you can combine upholstered and leather pieces to give the living room more layers and contrast. It seems men gravitate toward the masculine look of leather, while women choose softer fabrics and prints. This is a way to create a style that appeals to both sexes. Leather can be equally as elegant depending on the furniture style, so don't rule it out. It can look very distinctive on a wingback chair, mid-century sofa, cocktail ottoman and more. It's also a durable fabric that is a great choice if you have children.

Sofa/Chair/Ottoman

Another furniture grouping that works nicely is a combination of a sofa, chair and ottoman. Typically, an ottoman gets placed at the foot of the chair in close proximity, but I suggest that you separate the two pieces and place them on opposite sides of the sofa—coffee table in the center. It's a great layout for small living rooms that can't handle too many furniture pieces.

It still provides sufficient seating and creates a nice conversation cluster, which is when guests can comfortably engage in a conversation without the need to feel as if they are screaming from one side of the room to the other. The two woven stools were used in this layout to balance the scale of the sofa on the opposite side of the room. The round shape also breaks up all the straight lines found in the coffee table base, ottoman and sofa in the room.

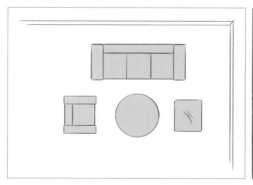

In bigger living rooms, you can double up on the chairs and ottomans on either side. By doing so, you are balancing the visual weight of the room. In this scenario, you can also use a longer bench instead of two ottomans since it fills up the same footprint. This makes it symmetrical with the width of the two chairs on the opposite side of the room. Scale and balance are two words I'll be using a lot throughout this book.

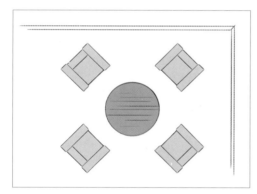

Lounge

Yet another furniture layout for a living room, which is increasing in popularity, is creating the look of a lounge by using four accent chairs as the main seating. Most homes have a family room and living room with a similar furniture grouping, which means the latter only gets used on special occasions. Instead, traditional living rooms are being converted into a lounge because it lends itself more for entertaining and overflow from the dining and kitchen areas. I love this look! The chairs can be grouped around a coffee table or ottoman and because the furniture typically floats in the center and not against the wall, the room appears to be more spacious. This look is inspired by commercial spaces such as hotels and restaurants, where you see different furniture groupings within the same space. The seating can all be the same style, which is classic, or a combination of armchairs with armless chairs; even ottomans can be mixed in for an eclectic grouping.

Before

Baby Friendly

You don't have to sacrifice style for safety when decorating your living room if you have small children. Yet, many parents seem to think so because their home resembles a playroom rather than a space meant for the entire family.

Understandably, you want to take every necessary precaution to avoid any potential safety hazard in your environment, but this doesn't mean the alternative is to live in an empty room either, as I've seen many times during initial consultations. I'm happy to report that there is a happy medium! The key is to not choose furniture with sharp corners, glass tops or fabrics that easily stain.

Around the time when babies start to crawl and toddlers begin to take their first steps is usually when nervous parents clear the room of furniture that might be dangerous. There are alternatives. For example, use an upholstered ottoman as a coffee table, which is softer to the touch. You can even find one that provides storage inside for toys and books. When choosing furniture, leather is a good option due to its durability, but you can also treat upholstered fabrics with a stain repellant or use a slipcover for easy maintenance. A great compromise is to look for furniture with new microfiber technology. It's a synthetic fiber that mimics the look of suede and leather and is also stain resistant. These tips also apply when you have fur babies—as I affectionately like to call pets.

Media Centers

A television is another key element in a living room. After all, it's usually the main reason we gravitate toward this space and hang out. Remember the days when we had a bulky television set encased in wood that doubled as furniture? And then it evolved into a gigantic projection screen television in our home? You're lucky if you're too young to remember, but I do because my parents had both at one point during my childhood. Now, of course, it's been replaced by streamlined flat-panel screens, and although we all agree they look much better, it can still be a challenge integrating them into our home's décor. Whether it's mounted directly on the wall or on top of a media center, they both scream, "Here I am!" and appear to be a black hole in the space.

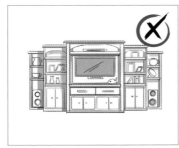

Create the look of a media center using shelves or artwork around the television instead of buying a pricey entertainment wall unit.

So, how do we work around this? In the makeover, the most effective and low-cost solution—literally $20—was to use a floating shelf the same width of the media console. This created the look of a built-in by framing the television above with the shelf and below with the console. By doing this, it also provided a display surface for other decorative accessories and collectibles.

Furniture stores still sell entertainment centers that surround the television with a matching TV stand, hutch, left and right bookcase piers, and left and right corner units. Personally, I feel the look is too heavy and can swallow up a room. The trend nowadays is for a simpler focal wall, whereby the television integrates with the overall styling of the living room without commanding too much attention with a massive entertaintment unit.

Different options to create the look of a media center on a budget include installing floating shelves on the wall surrounding the television. You can be symmetrical by repeating the same amount on both sides or do a combination of shelves and art to visually balance the wall; another suggestion is to only display artwork around the television, which disguises the flat screen within the gallery wall grouping. If you need more storage space, be open to the idea of using a server or credenza as a unique media base. You can also frame the television with open shelving units, which are always nice to display accessories in a living room.

Before

Accent Furniture

I can't say I've seen many TV trays used as side tables, but I have walked into many living rooms without end tables or sometimes even a coffee table, which makes the room feel incomplete. Although the main seating is comprised of sofas, ottomans and chairs, accent tables are the supporting pieces that make the room functional as well. It allows you to place an additional light source such as a lamp on an end table; or place a drink on a coffee table if you're entertaining family and friends in this main gathering area. These are great surfaces to decorate with books, candles and photo frames, too.

In the inspiration living room, I chose live-edge side tables with black hairpin legs, which are a perfect combination of rustic and industrial style. Live edge is the natural, raw edge of the wood once the tree is cut and the bark is removed. The side tables also tie in the wood planks on the accent wall.

Coffee tables come in all shapes and sizes—from square, rectangular and round and in materials such as wood, glass and metal; even ottomans can be used as coffee tables. The coffee table I chose combined hard and soft elements with a metal base and upholstered linen top. The raised table is modern and keeps the area open, which is a great trick to make a small space appear bigger. It is similar in effect to a glass-top coffee table, which creates the illusion of furniture that "is not really there" because it doesn't take up visual mass in the room.

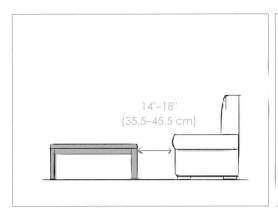

More Than Half

Coffee tables should be more than half the width of the sofa and allow 14 to 18 inches (35.5 to 45.5 cm) of space between the two furniture pieces.

When choosing a size, determine the area you have in front of the sofa in relation to the other furniture in the room and make sure the height of the coffee table is close to the seat height of the sofa. You want the coffee table to relate to all the surrounding furniture. Too small, it will look out of scale; too big, it will overpower the setting. You have to find the perfect balance, which, at the very least, should be more than half the width of the sofa. This is generally speaking, of course, so you have to trust your instincts on this one. The placement should be about 14 to 18 inches (35.5 to 45.5 cm) from the sofa, allowing enough room to walk around the table. This spacing applies mainly to a sofa since it relates directly to the coffee table in the forefront. For additional seating in the same layout, accent tables can be placed closer to a chair to set down a magazine or drink. If necessary, you can combine two identical pieces to form a bigger coffee table and even use pairings of smaller accent tables or ottomans for a modern twist.

The addition of two woven stools with wood legs is a whimsical accent that can be used for additional seating, but otherwise float in the room. They become sculptural and playful pieces within the décor. The reason I placed two of them side by side was to collectively fill the empty area in front of the window. Using only one would've been too weak, visually speaking, since their scale is minimal. The window and space also limited my choices. With the chaise sectional, I didn't have room for an accent chair, which would have blocked the view anyway. In design it's about knowing the alternatives and letting the room tell you what it needs.

Ottomans and stools come in different shapes and sizes and can replace basic seating. Traditionally, ottomans are grouped with a chair to function like a lounger, whereby you can sit and put your feet up. This is perfectly acceptable; just keep in mind that combining the two does take up more room, so make sure you have enough space. However, they are also used as stand-alone pieces in modern layouts. They are low to the ground, which keeps the space open, and are good options for small rooms. I use two ottomans in many of my designs when bigger furniture just won't work and I need to add enough seating. They are more effective in a living room when used in pairs to fill the footprint of the layout and make a bigger design statement.

3 Accessories

Whether you're a man or woman, an outfit is never truly complete without the accessories, right? This can include jewelry, tie, belt, shoes and a handbag—otherwise we still feel somewhat naked walking out the door. In design, it's not how much you spend on furniture that gives a room style; it's how you accessorize it that makes the difference.

This means that you can buy a $3,000 sofa for your living room, but if everything else around it is barren, the budget was not put to good use. I'd rather you spend less on large-scale basics and save money for the decorator details that will complete the living room. The chaise sectional in this makeover was $500 and is a perfect example of how you can still achieve a decorator look with an affordable price tag when you combine all three steps in the design process.

Decorative trays, books and candles make great accessories for a coffee table.

An area rug helps to visually group all the furniture in a room and ties in a color scheme.

Area Rug

The accessories in this living room finally made this house a home. I began with an 8 x 10-foot (2.5 x 3-m) area rug underneath the furniture grouping to define the space and balance out the scale of the sectional. The rug has an old-world pattern in a subdued color palette of blues and grays. It complemented the paint color and contrasted nicely against the darker gray sofa. Keep in mind that using too much of the same color in a room will make it visually flat. The goal is to add different colors and textures to create layers. An area rug is also a good starting point to build the color scheme of the room as you pull those tones onto other accessories such as throw pillows and artwork. The different shades of blue throw pillows on the sofa were pulled from the area rug as well. The pop of yellow is an unexpected color, yet it ties in with the wood plank wall. I believe color combinations work best in threes to give a room dimension. In this living room, it was a color story of gray, blue and yellow.

Don't be afraid to layer your rugs either. It reflects a more eclectic, bohemian chic style and can look great on the floor. This works best when you combine a much larger solid or braided area rug as the base in natural fibers, similar to a jute or sisal, and then place a smaller rug on a diagonal on top with a pattern/texture to add a vintage look to your décor.

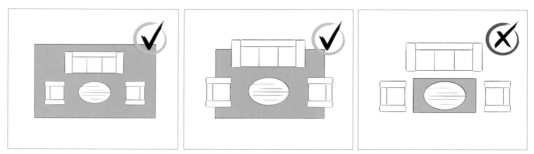

An area rug needs to be in balance with the furniture grouping and the size of the actual room.

Size of Area Rug

The size of the area rug you choose can totally make or break the design. The most popular sizes for living rooms are 5 x 8 feet (1.5 x 2.5 m), 8 x 10 feet (2.5 x 3 m) or 9 x 12 feet (2.7 x 3.7 m). They are a great layering piece to accent a furniture grouping and add warmth over tile or wood floors. What size to choose really depends on the amount of furniture in the room. At the very minimum it should be bigger than the sofa; however, if you have a loveseat or accent chair as part of the grouping, the rug should be big enough for the front feet of the furniture to be placed over them. This creates an anchor in the space that ties all the furniture pieces together in the living room. If you go too small, then the other furniture around it feels almost disconnected. I know it sounds crazy, but trust me on this.

Depending on the size of the room, you can certainly go bigger and place all the furniture completely on the area rug. This will be a matter of preference, but you certainly need to have ample space or you'll end up looking like you have wall-to-wall carpeting instead and the area rug will overpower the living room. There should be at least 24 inches (61 cm) in distance between the area rug and wall in large rooms, and between 12 to 18 inches (30.5 to 45.5 cm) in smaller spaces.

Area rugs come in many shapes as well. A good rule of thumb is to have it mimic the shape of the room and the width of the furniture arrangement, which in many cases is rectangular. For narrow rooms, a square area rug might be better suited. If the furniture is floating in the center of the room in a circular pattern—similar to a lounge grouping—then a round shape would be the best option. Once again, make sure the circumference is big enough to either place all the furniture on the rug or at least the front legs of the main furniture to make it all tie together. These are the same rules you follow when placing a rectangular area rug.

Lighting

I love the table lamps in the feature makeover because they appear to be sculptural elements on the side tables, yet are a functional light source. The metal silhouette of a lamp base appeals to the architectural details the husband likes—almost like an art piece. The rectangular lamp shade also complements the look. Lots of style for only $30 a lamp!

For symmetrical reasons, I used the exact lamp on each of the side tables. However, it's also possible to use a combination of floor lamp on one side of the sofa and a table lamp on the other to break up the symmetry. Yet another option on trend is to use two floor lamps: one on either side of the sofa. If you do this, make sure the side table is not too wide, though. This works best with accent tables, which are a smaller scale, so as not to overcrowd the area.

Don't be afraid to mix floor and table lamps on either side of a sofa for an eclectic style.

Throw Pillows

Nowadays, even though a new sofa may come with coordinating decorative pillows, I still suggest you incorporate other throw pillows in different textures, solids and patterns to create a look all your own. You can pull accent colors from the inspiration piece in the room onto the sofa and accent chairs. However, be careful not to overpower the furniture with too many pillows. It's important to also take into consideration the size and fill.

Before

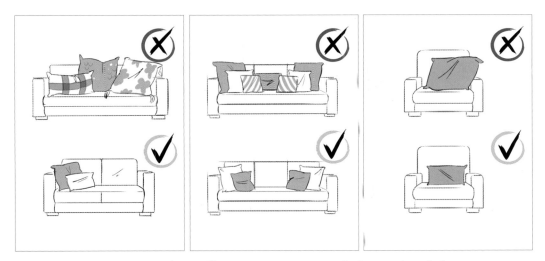

The wrong size or too many throw pillows can overpower a sofa, love seat or chair.

As in a bedroom suite, my favorite fill is down feathers. You can sit on and squish the pillows as many times as you want and with some fluffing they look good as new. As a designer my pet-peeve is seeing a sad-looking "pancake pillow" from being sat on numerous times stuffed with polyester fiberfill. Besides, how else are you going to achieve the "karate-chop" look like you see in decorator magazines if you don't use down-filled pillows? Of course, I'm teasing as this is really a matter of personal preference, but I must admit to being a light chop pillow addict to achieve a tailored look.

A standard 18-inch (45.5-cm) square pillow works well on most sofas and you can layer the look with smaller sizes and shapes. Combine pillows with large patterns against small patterns so they don't compete; mix in solids with an accent color you wish to highlight that is found in the room. In the living room featured, I pulled from the blue found in the stools and also yellows, which brought out the wood tones on the plank wall.

Exactly how many throw pillows you use on a sofa really depends on the length. On an average sofa (measuring 86 inches [218.5 cm]) I would use four pillows maximum—placing two in each corner. On a love seat (measuring 60 inches [152.5 cm]) I would use only two and place them together on the same side. Sectionals can handle a maximum of five or six pillows—two on each end and then a couple in the center corner. On an armchair or accent chair (measuring 35 inches [89 cm] wide) I would use one throw pillow, but the shape will depend on the style and height of the chair itself. If the chair is low-back and upholstered, a rectangular throw pillow will look better. Not every accent chair needs a throw pillow, though—especially if the style is a timeless classic such as mid-century. In this case, the chair is a design feature in the living room that you don't wish to cover up. It is one of those times where you have to trust your instincts to see if the pillow will complement or overpower the chair.

If you love the look of throws or blankets in a living room like I do, then consider the pattern as well when you're mixing in the decorative pillows. I used a graphic chevron in yellow, gray and white that coordinates back to the throw pillows on the chaise sectional. Throws are used in decorating to add color, texture and warmth. They make the room more inviting and give it a lived-in feeling, which is the goal with every space I design. It's about creating a style that has a casual elegance.

Window Treatments

Finally, don't forget to accessorize the walls and windows. These serve as the backdrop to your space, so they must be addressed accordingly. Curtains are not just used for privacy; they are also considered another style layer in the room. The window treatments I chose for this living room have grommets on top and are in a dark gray, woven matelassé fabric. This means it has a stitched pattern, so the panels have an interesting texture. I wanted contrast, but at the same time I didn't want any bold color or print to compete with the wood plank wall. These grommet panels against the wall color give a tone-on-tone effect, which complements the living room setting.

The Art of a Tablescape

When it comes down to the details of decorating a room, a question I often get is, "How do I arrange everything on an accent table to make it look pretty . . . like you see in the magazines?"

Well, the term we use in the decorating world is creating a tablescape or vignette, which basically means a small, decorative arrangement or grouping of items that are pleasing to the eye. In most cases, it's on top of a table, but it can also include merchandising shelves, bookcases and even furniture groupings together. In a much broader sense, it can also apply to how we set the dining table, but for our purposes let's concentrate on smaller surfaces such as end tables or coffee tables.

Some rules you should keep in mind when creating your vignette is that you want to vary the height of the objects (high and low), group things usually in threes, and for the most part, display items that relate to each other for a stronger visual presentation. The purpose is to make the eye linger a few moments as it travels up and down across the vignette, appreciating all the items.

Group objects in threes and vary the heights to create a pleasant display on your coffee or side table.

On the coffee table in the feature makeover I used a round tray to group a candleholder, a bowl with spheres and a starburst metal sculpture. Then I placed some oversized art books off to the side, which make the perfect décor accessory on a coffee table—hence the name coffee table books. On the end tables, a small plant, family photo and decorative box complete the look next to the lamp. If you have a larger coffee table, the goal is to make a statement in each corner. Group similar objects together, stack books, a vase with flowers and candleholders are the go-to items. Avoid the clutter of placing too many small knick-knacks all over the surface. A great tip if you have smaller objects is to use books and decorative boxes to elevate them and give them more presence. The storage boxes are great to hide those remote controls.

In any tablescape, the goal is to display a grouping of collectibles to create a scene or story that expresses the homeowner's interests. It's a perfect opportunity to make a design statement and also refresh the décor on the table by season.

Wall art looks better when it is proportional to the width of the sofa and this can be achieved with a large, single frame or a collection of frames.

Artwork

In a living room, a blank wall over the sofa is usually the main canvas to hang art. If the area is big, don't hang art too small. It will look disproportionate. The general rule is the art above the sofa should be two-thirds the width of the sofa. You can make a statement with an oversized frame or group a collection of individual frames to create a stronger focal point. Don't be afraid to mix a variety of items such as frames, canvases and even three dimensional objects to tell your story.

In the living room makeover, I used the wood plank wall as my main artwork in the space. However, I still took advantage of the empty walls on either side by adding photo ledges and leaning matted frames of typography prints the husband created, who is a graphic artist, for a casual display. The prints were used as part of their wedding décor, so it truly told the story of their lives in the space. On the other side, a simple reclaimed wood frame with the words "Live, Laugh, Love" expresses the couple's philosophy about life. It's art with a personal connection to the homeowners.

On the opposite wall, I continued personalizing the décor with their initials in marquee letters that combined wood and metal. It was the perfect mix of his and her and the rustic/industrial style they both liked. It was a fun element in the living room.

Design Your Life

You know that feeling you get when you receive fresh flowers? It is a thoughtful gesture by someone who loves and appreciates you, and it makes you feel special. Well, you can design a moment like this that brings you inner joy by having an arrangement of flowers greet you when you walk into your living room. It's a simple concept, but not too many homeowners take the time to do this for themselves. Of course, it would be great if we can pick beautiful flowers from our own garden, but most of us don't have a green thumb or a garden for that matter. The next best thing is to purchase flowers, but this doesn't have to be an expensive bouquet from a florist by any means.

Become your own floral designer by making arrangements with flowers you can buy at a farmers' market or grocery store. I promise, it's not hard. Use a clear vase in a modern shape (square or rectangle) and wrap the inside surface with foliage that covers the entire circumference—you can overlap leaves if necessary. Just make sure the size is big enough to hide the stems of the flowers. Cut the stems, so the flower sits about 1 inch (2.5 cm) above the height of the vase and arrange the buds tightly inside. When you're done, you have the look of an expensive professional arrangement for a fraction of the cost. Choose your favorite flowers or use a single stem in a unique bud vase. The point is you deserve to gift yourself with this moment and not wait for a special occasion. Flowers are said to be nature's gifts, and adding them in your living room environment will make it a happier home. Feel-good decorating!

Before

Wood Planked Walls

Are you ready to give a plain wall niche in your living room a makeover? It's amazing how by changing one element in a space we can make an impact on the overall look of the room.

Barn wood accent walls are a big design trend in home décor. It adds a warm and rustic look that complements any decorating style, from farmhouse to modern, and is a great way to create a focal point in any space. It's also an easy DIY project you can do to save money and give your home a lot of bang for your buck.

It can define a living room as a backdrop to the sofa as seen in our inspiration makeover, but it can also be used in a dining room behind a sideboard, as a headboard in a bedroom, and really anywhere you wish to add texture on the walls and make a statement.

For smaller areas you can recycle wood pallets, but for larger surfaces you're better off buying new materials at a home improvement store and distressing it yourself. There are different looks you can achieve with this trend, and it really depends on your preference. For example, you can mix different size boards for a more random pattern or even use wood plank flooring material on the wall. It's really up to you!

Materials

Measuring tape

1" x 4" (2.5 x 10-cm) pine

Table saw (optional)

Miter box and saw (optional)

Disposable gloves

Wood stain—water based/color of your choice

Cloth rags

Nail gun

Level

Steps

1. Begin by measuring the wall you wish to cover in the wood. Measure the height and width. Go to your local home improvement store and buy the wood planks necessary. I used 1 x 4-inch (2.5 x 10-cm) untreated pine wood. This can be purchased by the foot or in standard lengths of 8 feet (2.5 m). The home improvement store can also cut the wood for you as long as you give them the measurements. If not, you can easily do this at home with a table saw, but if you don't feel confident handling electrical tools, a miter box with saw kit will do the job, too.

2. Using gloves, apply stain with the cloth rags in a color of your choice. Try different stain colors on the boards to create depth in the pattern once installed on the wall. In the project featured, two stain colors were used—a gray and a brown tone. If you wish to reveal more of the wood grain, wipe off some of the stain shortly after application or use sand paper. You can also dilute the stain with mineral spirits.

3. To install the wood planks on the wall, I used an air compressor-powered nail gun, but a cordless brad nailer will also work. You can rent these tools at a home improvement store. Since the wood boards are 1 inch (2.5 cm) thick, use 2-inch (5-cm) finish nails in the nailer. Finish nails are sunk or submerged into the wood to hide them from view. You can also paint over them, making them hardly noticeable.

4. Begin by installing the first row of boards closest to the floor and make sure it is straight by using a level tool. Any variation will be obvious as you reach further up the wall, so it's important this first row be completely level. The trick is to shoot the nail in different directions on the board—angled up and down—to secure it to the wall.

5. Stagger the joints of the boards to create a random pattern, and cut the boards to size using the table saw or miter box with saw kit. Notice some rows are comprised of two boards, while others have three. You can also cut around any outlets if necessary. Proceed with the wood wall installation using a nail gun until you reach the top of the wall.

6. Once the wood is installed, you can appreciate the subtle differences in the stain. I went for a weathered gray finish, which complemented the flooring in the room. However, you can also stain it darker if that is your preference. The secret is to use different stain colors to add depth and contrast—unless you prefer to have a uniform finish, which can look more modern.

After

The wall niche becomes a beautiful focal point in the living room covered in wood planks. It's rustic but also modern and was easily done in one day for less than $200 for materials. Special thanks to Danny from Carved Woodworks for his help with this project.

Before

CHAPTER 3

Bedroom Suites
Create Your Own Personal Sanctuary That Appeals to All Your Senses

A bedroom suite is more than just a room to sleep. It's a sanctuary from the stresses of everyday life where you can rest and reenergize your spirit. When you open your bedroom door, you should feel as if you're about to experience something special that is as beautiful as it is comfortable.

Often times, I find that homeowners leave their bedroom as a last priority when they decorate because no one really "sees" this room. They can shut the door and it's out of sight, out of mind. I believe it is quite the opposite. You, the homeowner, see this room every day and every night. It should be considered one of the most important rooms in your home since you literally spend one-third of your lifetime sleeping (based on an average night's sleep of eight hours a day). A bedroom deserves your full attention from the beginning because it has a direct effect on how you begin and end your day.

We've all heard the saying, "you are what you eat"; well, when it comes to home décor, how the rooms look says a lot about you, too. In the inspiration room, the space had lots of potential, but the homeowner was at a loss not knowing where to begin. She knew she didn't like the current furniture and wanted to update the look. She was frustrated and unhappy because she felt stuck in the past and wasn't fully enjoying the present. I always begin by analyzing first what doesn't work in a room and, unfortunately, that meant all the furniture had to go. The three things that worked in the room were the paint color, the mattress and the bedding, so at least we had something, right?

1 Walls

Does your bedroom feel like a retreat when you close the door? It should be a space you look forward to unwinding in at the end of the day. If not, the color palette could have a lot to do with why you're not finding rest and relaxation. Paint colors can dramatically change not only the look, but the mood in a bedroom. If your current bedroom walls are white because you're afraid of making a bold color choice, you really don't have to go too far outside your comfort zone. My recommendation is to choose a creamy shade of off-white, taupe or gray to add warmth in the space. I know this is still keeping it safe, but by choosing a soothing color palette for the walls, you at least eliminate the stark whiteness of the room, which can make a space feel sterile and cold. White walls also have a tendency to make a room feel unfinished—unless it complements a modern style of decorating.

In the bedroom suite, the silver gray color was romantic and the perfect backdrop for the new furniture. When choosing a paint color for the bedroom, I find that a good source of inspiration is the bedding. This makes sense since the bed is always the focal point, and bedding is an integral part of what makes it inviting. It's the one furniture piece that defines the purpose of the bedroom—similar to a dining table in the dining room and a sofa in a living room. As a result, you want the bedding to coordinate with the overall color scheme. If your bedding has different colors, the best thing to do is pick an accent color in the background of the fabric and have that be your paint inspiration for the walls. This will ensure you have a cohesive color story in the end. Too much of the same hue in a space can make the décor look flat and repetitive.

Paint Colors for a Bedroom

Good choices for bedrooms are cool shades of soft blue, green and gray, along with neutral shades of cream and taupe to create a relaxing spa-like atmosphere. I tend to stay away from bright and bold colors because they give off too much energy, especially when you're completely surrounded on all four walls. You can still add pops of color on your bedding and accents throughout the room, but the background should have a calming effect, which promotes rest and relaxation. Another benefit of having a softer and neutral palette on the walls is that you can always change out your bedding and accessories to redecorate the room in the future.

If you still have the desire to go darker, green and violet work well in a variety of bedroom styles like modern, traditional or eclectic. They are cool colors that remind us of water and sky, even ice and snow, whereas warm colors remind us of heat and sunshine. Although red is a warm color, it can also be considered in moderation. We all know it represents the color of love and passion, and one would think it's a natural choice for a bedroom, but it can be very overwhelming. Choose a red with a muted tone, which means it's not a pure color similar to a fire-engine red. Instead it has gray added, so the color gets slightly darker, softer and cooler. This is the correct way to do red in a bedroom and can work on an accent wall. Yellow is another tricky color, so go for softer shades, not brighter.

Once you decide on a paint color, make sure you take into consideration the size of the bedroom and also the lighting conditions when choosing the intensity of the color. Lighter shades can make a room feel more spacious as it visually makes the walls recess, which is a great design tip for small bedrooms. While darker colors tend to close in the walls, it can work in your favor if you're dealing with an extremely large bedroom and you want to create a cozier setting. A good rule of thumb is that if your wall color draws more attention than the overall room design, there's a problem. Wall color, furnishings and accessories should all complement each other to create a harmonious environment.

The Fifth Wall

Ceilings can be considered the fifth wall in a bedroom and for the most part, I like painting them as well. Why stare at a white canvas lying in bed? If you tend to gravitate to darker wall colors, then I recommend painting the ceiling two shades lighter. And if you like softer colors on the walls, then consider one shade darker for the ceiling. This is called a monochromatic color scheme, which creates a cohesive, yet subtle distinction between the walls and ceiling that will complement the rest of the decorating layers that will be added later by way of furniture and accessories.

I especially like painting ceilings when they have a beautiful architectural feature worthy of highlighting such as a tray ceiling, which is a recessed or inverted ceiling used to create a sense of additional height in a bedroom; or when the bedroom has crown molding. Whatever the case may be in your own home, be open to the idea of painting a ceiling as it makes a statement in any bedroom—similar to a cozy blanket wrapping you on all sides. The ceiling in the inspiration bedroom was painted a metallic gray, which is a darker version of the wall color.

Choosing the proper scale and amount of furniture based on the size of the room is an integral part of the design process in a bedroom.

2 Furniture

Clutter comes in many forms. It's not just attributed to scattered papers or untidy clothes. It can also be furniture that impedes your movement in a bedroom from either being bulky or having too many pieces. Can you relate to this? The goal should be to create a feeling of order and spaciousness that frees up the "visual" clutter and, as a result, becomes a space that feels like a sanctuary for you.

The most exciting part of any makeover is choosing new furniture, but this moment can also be overwhelming. The size of the furniture needs to be in balance with the size of the room. This means that if you have a spacious bedroom, don't choose furniture that is too small or too few pieces. The bedroom will still look empty as a result. And vice-versa: if you're decorating a tiny bedroom, massive furniture like canopy or sleigh beds and oversized nightstands will make the room appear even smaller. The scale of the furniture plays a big role in your room design.

Mattress Size

One of the most common mistakes begins initially with the selection of the mattress size. I know the tendency is to think "bigger is better", which is why a king-size bed is most popular. I completely understand, but you have to be realistic and choose the size that works best with the dimensions of the bedroom. A king-size bed in a small bedroom will dwarf the actual size of the room. Yes, you will have ample space on the mattress to sleep on, but it's not a good design choice if you don't have any space whatsoever to walk around the bed or place other essential furniture pieces next to it, like a nightstand. The idea that a king-size bed is the epitome of comfort is a myth. The most popular mattress size for a couple of average height is a queen size bed, which is only 16 inches (40.5 cm) less in width from a king (basically 8 inches [20.5 cm] less for each person). Be mindful of this because the right mattress size along with the rest of the décor in your bedroom work together to nurture the mind, body and spirit, which results in a restful night's sleep.

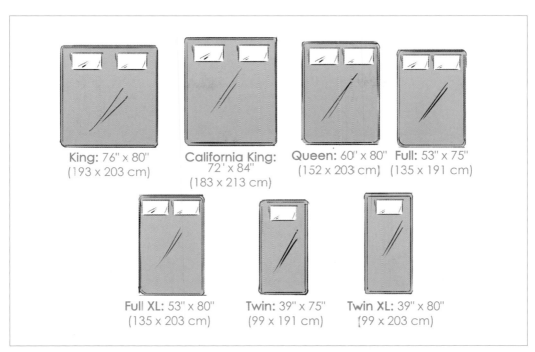

King: 76" x 80"
(193 x 203 cm)

California King:
72' x 84"
(183 x 213 cm)

Queen: 60' x 80"
(152 x 203 cm)

Full: 53" x 75"
(135 x 191 cm)

Full XL: 53" x 80"
(135 x 203 cm)

Twin: 39" x 75"
(99 x 191 cm)

Twin XL: 39" x 80"
(99 x 203 cm)

Not only does a mattress need to be comfortable for sleeping, but you also have to consider the size of the bedroom.

This is much harder to achieve when the wrong mattress size is working against you before you even begin to decorate. Avoid this mistake by differentiating between what you want and what the bedroom space can handle. The bed should have at least 2 to 3 feet (61 to 91.5 cm) of walking room all the way around. Be mindful of placing the bed too close to doors swinging into or out of the room. The inspiration room had a spacious floor plan, so the king-size bed was the perfect scale.

Ideally, the bed should be placed on the feature wall opposite the bedroom door. It becomes the immediate focal point as you enter the room. If your wall happens to have a window in the center, don't be discouraged. It is okay to place a bed on a window wall—especially if you have no other options. I admit it will look more in balance if the window happens to be the same width as the bed, but if that's not the case, there are decorating tricks you can do to create the illusion of visual symmetry. You can easily extend the curtain rod outside the window frame or drape the entire wall from side to side in curtains, which also creates a dramatic backdrop to the bed.

Before

With this in mind, now the fun can begin. The furniture selection is one of my favorite parts about this bedroom suite makeover. Most people would go to a furniture store to shop for a complete bedroom set. Personally, I like to create a more custom look by mixing pieces from different collections; that is exactly what a designer does to make the space personal to the client.

Bed

In any bedroom, but especially in a bedroom suite, the headboard is the star of the room. I prefer going tall whenever possible to make a statement. I broke up all the wood furniture by choosing a tufted upholstered headboard in a gray linen fabric. It's beautiful and elegant. Like the mattress size, you have to take into consideration your square footage in relation to the style and scale of the furniture. In smaller spaces, four-poster and sleigh beds can be very romantic, but they can definitely overpower a small bedroom by obstructing the sight lines. In many cases you can achieve a similar look by removing the footboard or switching to a platform style that sits lower to the ground and will make the bedroom appear larger.

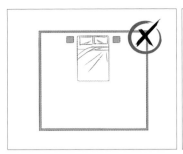  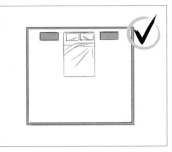

Nightstands add symmetry and choosing a size depends on two factors: size of the actual bed and how much space you have to work with.

An ideal height for a nightstand is level with the top of the mattress.

Nightstands

Nightstands are important in all bedroom designs because they anchor and balance the bed on the feature wall. It's okay to keep it traditional by using matching nightstands, but you can also add a bit more personality and create a look all your own. Don't be afraid to combine different shapes and styles like a round with a rectangular. The key to making it work is to keep the same height and width, and be consistent with either the finish or color. In the bedroom suite, the design details set them apart, yet the look is still cohesive because they have the same wood finish. Nightstands should also be functional with features such as drawers that provide storage near the bed for books, eyeglasses or remotes. The ideal depth is about 25 inches (63.5 cm) or less, which is enough to accommodate a table lamp, alarm clock and accessories, and the height should be about the same level as the top of the mattress or slightly higher.

Generally speaking, the size of the nightstand should be proportional to the size of the bed. If you have a king-size bed, which occupies a lot of visual weight in the bedroom, placing a small pedestal table next to it might look out of balance. However, this really depends on the actual space you have to work with on either side between the bed and the wall. The more space you have, the wider the nightstand can be to balance the scale of the bed. Nightstands can vary in sizes, but a standard width is around 18 inches (45.5 cm) for a smaller style. For bigger beds like a king size, you can even consider a chest of drawers, which range in size from 30 to 40 inches (76 to 101.5 cm) wide.

Shopping for Style

Furniture is a big expense, so be conscious of your budget and don't feel the pressure to purchase everything in one place. It's okay to comparison shop and mix high- and low-priced furniture to achieve an affordable style. Splurge where it matters most, like the bed frame and mattress, and save with the rest of the pieces. A great resource for accent furniture is discounted home stores. I probably buy about 50 percent or more of my furnishings at these retailers for a room makeover. They carry everything from side tables to benches, and why pay full price somewhere else when you don't have to? Don't close yourself off to furniture that might require assembly either. I've assembled so many pieces in my career, which can be tedious, but it's worth it to get the look for less. Often times you also have to think out of the box when you're working with a tight budget and explore non-traditional furnishings that will still give you the same function. For example, floating shelves can also work as nightstands in a modern setting! Install them at the same height as the top of the mattress on either side of the bed and it's an economical and space-saving solution. The depth of the shelf can work with a sleek study lamp or you can also install a swivel arm light fixture on the wall above it as a light source next to the bed. There is always a solution to any challenge, and I promise it will look great!

Visual Weight of Furniture

It's best to distribute the visual weight of the furniture equally throughout the bedroom (and in all spaces) and this is achieved when the scale of the furniture is in balance with the size of the wall it is placed on. This means to try not to place two heavy pieces of furniture like a dresser/mirror combo and a chest of drawers next to each other on the same wall because it can look overcrowded. Ideally, each wall should have one piece of furniture in front of it and this relates back to the concept of having negative space, which brings balance to a room by creating a visual separation between one thing and the next. Another example is placing a wide dresser on a narrow wall, which was actually a design dilemma I faced when I first saw the bedroom suite. The visual weight of the furniture overpowered the wall and the area look cluttered even though it was only one piece of furniture. By choosing a tall chest of drawers instead, the wall is now in

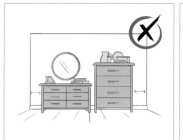

Placing too much furniture on the same wall can visually clutter a bedroom. If possible, try to separate the pieces, so that each wall has its own moment.

balance with the furniture. These are subtle details that make all the difference in design. If storage is an issue, my suggestion is to maximize your closet space by investing in a good organizing system. It's worth every penny since it offsets the cost of having to buy additional furniture for your clothes that can otherwise clutter your bedroom. Another solution is to consider placing the dresser or chest of drawers inside the closet to free up valuable floor space.

Seating Area

There are different ways to add a seating area in a bedroom, so don't feel discouraged if you don't have an expansive space like the inspiration room. By placing the loveseat and ottoman at the foot of the bed, I was able to create a multifunctional space within the bedroom for watching television or reading a book. It becomes like a lounge setting near the fireplace for the homeowners, which makes the experience feel like a true hotel suite. The reason this works is because, first and foremost, I had the space to do it in front of the bed and the size of the furniture doesn't overpower the bed or the room. The loveseat fits within the width of the king bed—anything bigger than that would've been the wrong scale—and it's also lower than the bed, so it doesn't create a visual wall that might block it otherwise. It's best to keep the fabric solid on large furniture pieces because you can always add texture and color with throw pillows to complement any bedding you have. I kept the fabric choices very monochromatic because I wanted this area to blend with the rest of the bedroom.

Another grouping that can work at the foot of the bed is a pair of accent chairs with an ottoman, which opens up the space. Ottomans are a great choice because you can use them as a footstool or tea table, so it's a versatile accent piece in the room. The gray leather cocktail ottoman that I used was a clearance find for only $70. Either grouping works well at the foot of the bed, near a window or in a separate area within the bedroom to function as a cozy den—provided you have adequate space.

For smaller bedrooms, an upholstered bench is also practical for seating and even storage. You can also create a perfect reading nook by placing a chair and ottoman in one corner of your bedroom. Small accent tables near the seating arrangement are practical to keep your favorite book nearby and a place for your coffee in the morning as you experience a quiet moment in your bedroom retreat.

3 Accessories

At first impression, you might think accessorizing a bedroom refers to the small décor items that we place on a dresser or nightstand. It can certainly apply, but the broader meaning refers to the layers of design details that will make your space inviting and created especially for you. Think of them as individual "happy moments" within the bedroom that collectively bring your spirit joy.

There are ways to capture this feeling in a bedroom to make it look more luxurious without paying high prices. The secret is to do your homework and know what to look for when you shop. For example, do you really know what "thread count" means when you shop for bed sheets? It can make a world of difference. It all begins with the bed, which sets the tone of the room from the moment you open the door. The mix of textures, patterns and colors are the layers that give the room its personal style.

Bedding

It's fair to say most homeowners are drawn to comforter sets because they make it very easy and affordable to achieve a coordinated look for the bedding. Be careful, though, as sometimes too coordinated can look novice—like a repetitive theme. It's okay to use a basic set as the inspiration for the design and color scheme, but you can personalize the bedding for a custom ensemble when the time comes to dress the bed.

In the inspiration makeover, I kept the original bedding, but the different accents give it a new look. The main body of the bed now features a solid gray coverlet with a subtle sheen to create a more glamorous vibe. The material is elegant enough for her, and the color appeals to him. Adding a coverlet is a simple way to create layers in your bedding because it allows you to fold the comforter or duvet at the foot of the bed. Duvets are especially great to update the look of a comforter without having to buy a new one. It functions like one large pillowcase.

It seems one of the biggest challenges is finding bedding that isn't too feminine for the man or too plain for the woman. The compromise would be to combine solids and patterns. For a modern style, create a monochromatic color scheme and combine darker and lighter shades of the same color on the bedding. Then add a pattern with the bed sheets and throw pillows. More dominant patterns are okay, but it works best when you balance them with solids. The idea is not to make the bedding look too busy. It should be simple and inviting to help you unwind at the end of the day.

Fabrics & Thread Count

Thread count refers to the number of threads woven together in a square inch, both vertically and horizontally. Imagine your comforter or bed sheet divided into a grid of small 1 x 1-inch (2.5 x 2.5-cm) squares. The higher the thread count in each grid, the tighter the weave, and as a result the overall fabric will feel finer and softer. That's why the price increases as the thread count is higher. Better-quality sheets come in at 200 thread count or higher. Among the most popular and softer are 100 percent cotton sheets such as Egyptian and pima cottons.

Choose fabrics and materials that are soft to the touch and can breathe throughout the night. Fabrics of 100 percent cotton are the best selection and are used in a variety of bed sheets, duvets, comforters, blankets, coverlets and pillows. I would stay away from synthetic and acrylic fibers, which do not absorb moisture as well and increase body temperature, resulting in a less comfortable sleep I'm a big fan of down comforters and pillows because it gives you the sensation of being cradled in luxury. But if you suffer from allergies, look for labels that say "hypo-allergenic" and "down alternative." Finally, I also suggest that you purchase a mattress pad and a pillow cover with a zipper that helps protect against stains and dust mites. Aside from the actual furniture, the mattress is another essential investment for any bedroom, so it's worth prolonging its use.

Throw Pillows

The decorative pillows are everything on a bed—and I'm not referring to the rectangular pillow shams that typically coordinate with the comforter set. Additionally, I like using euro shams as the first layer in dressing the bed. These are larger, 26 x 26-inch (66 x 66-cm) pillows usually placed behind standard-, queen- and king-sized pillows to accessorize a bed. Three euro shams are needed on a king bed to balance the width of the headboard; queen and full sizes can work well with two. Euro shams are not an absolute, but they can definitely give your bed a luxurious look. In front of euro shams, place the sleeping pillows, followed by the decorative shams and throw pillows.

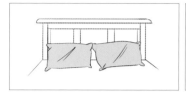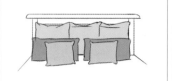

Throw pillows give a bedroom a welcoming and luxurious look. Place the largest against the headboard and go down in size as you dress the bed.

As the eye travels from high to low, I finished dressing the bed with throw pillows that accent the bedding. I used a total of six in different sizes because a king-size bed has more surface area, but it's really a matter of preference. At the very minimum, three throw pillows should be used on a king-size bed.

Monogrammed and pillows with typography are all the rage in home décor, and it's a great way to add a whimsical detail on your bed, too. In my opinion, throw pillows are like jewelry on a bed. Without them the bed would be too plain. I know women understand this, but some men, on the other hand, seem to find too many pillows on a bed a bit excessive. I think their biggest complaint is not knowing what to do with the pillows when they go to sleep. It's a legitimate question; my job as a designer is to find the perfect balance between style and function to please both sexes. A simple solution is to use a bench at the foot of the bed to place the pillows in before going to bed. There's always a design solution for everything.

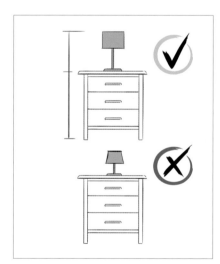

The height of the lamp needs to visually balance the size of the bedside table.

Lighting

A combination of lamps and chandeliers are needed to set the right mood in a bedroom. It's just as important as the color scheme of the room to enhance the atmosphere. In the inspiration room, the six-light geometric chandelier was grand in scale, but it still looked light and elegant in the bedroom. I didn't want anything heavy that would take away from the beautiful ceiling treatment. There are many styles of chandeliers to consider, from a crystal chandelier for a glamorous look to an oversized drum shade pendant for a modern aesthetic, so this is really a matter of preference; but my suggestion is to choose a hanging fixture (i.e., pendant or chandelier style) over the bed, which definitely makes more of a statement.

Lamps on the nightstands are equally important in the lighting plan because they are part of the feature wall that frames the bed. They are both decorative and functional when placed on a nightstand. A mistake I often see homeowners make is buying the wrong scale lamp for the size of the nightstand. Have you noticed by now how scale is a factor in every design decision? A lamp should not overpower the nightstand and vice-versa. As a general guideline, a lamp should not be more than 1.5 times taller than the surface it is sitting on, and the lampshade's diameter should be smaller than the width of the table. Keeping these measurements in mind will ensure the height and width of the lamp will be proportional to the size of the nightstand.

Mirrors

The majority of the mirrors that I see in bedrooms are a matching set with the dresser. Although you see it as part of the collection at the furniture store, don't feel obligated to purchase it because there are other alternatives that might be less expensive. Having a mirror attached to a dresser can make the piece look very heavy in a space—especially when it has a thick, wood frame in the same finish as the dresser. Ask yourself this question: Do I really use the mirror on the dresser? I find that the bathroom mirrors are more functional in the household, so the dresser mirrors become obsolete. You can save yourself the cost of the mirror, which can be around $200 to $300, and only buy the dresser. Yes, you can separate the pieces and not buy the two together. From a design perspective, use the space above the dresser for artwork or a collection of frames; or if you would like a mirror, opt for a different style and finish that doesn't match the dresser that you can purchase from a discount home store at a fraction of the cost. The mirror becomes artwork as a stand-alone piece on the wall when it's not part of a matching set.

Artwork

The artwork in a bedroom should tie back to the color scheme you're using in a similar manner to the paint and bedding inspiration. I know artwork is personal, but I prefer when the wall décor is part of the background in the overall design and does not overpower the space with too much print and color. For this reason, a good choice is images of nature or classic black-and-white photos of special moments in your life. Create a beautiful collage of matted photos within different picture frame sizes on one wall in your bedroom highlighting your wedding, family and/or vacations. The images will bring a smile to your face every time you look at them—morning and night—a subtle reminder of what's truly important in life: to live a life well-lived.

Artwork doesn't have to be expensive either. The prints I used above the bed were created by simply framing metallic wallpaper remnants, which I had left over from another job. This was a great way to stretch the decorating dollar and create abstract art. The wall area above a bed can be tricky because you don't want the art to compete. It should all work in harmony as the focal point. I find that sculptural elements like decorative mirrors and wall décor in sets of threes are good options as accents above a bed.

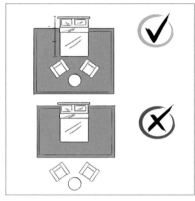

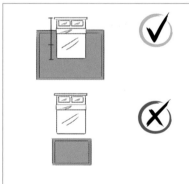

Choosing the proper area rug size and placement is important to define a bedroom. Allow for the rug to extend ⅔ underneath the bed and for any seating near the front to be grouped on top.

Area Rugs

An area rug in a bedroom is another layer that can add a luxurious touch. It can define the bed and seating arrangement with rich texture and softness to walk on with bare feet. I prefer neutrals because it can work with any color scheme, but it doesn't mean you have to necessarily keep it solid. In the inspiration room, the gray pattern and shag textures are details that give the floor more visual interest and contrast nicely with the solid fabrics on the furniture.

To make an impact and define the bed in the center of the room, it's best to extend an area rug from the bottom two-thirds of the bed. If you have a seating arrangement at the foot of the bed, then pull the rug forward, so the furniture sits entirely on the rug, while still keeping it slightly underneath the bed as well. This helps to unify the whole grouping. Choose the appropriate area rug size to accomplish this. In most cases, an average 10 x 10-foot (3 x 3-m) bedroom will accommodate a 5 x 8-foot (1.5 x 2.5-m) area rug. If the bedroom is much wider, consider going up to an 8 x 10-foot (2.5 x 3-m) size to cover more of the floor and balance the size of the room.

Window Treatments

The ability to control natural light in a bedroom is also a key factor in getting a good night's rest. Therefore, window treatments play a huge role in bedroom décor since they must be both functional and decorative. Bright areas are great in the morning, but not so much at night if you have a light post or landscape lighting right outside your window. Choosing curtain panels that are double-lined or blackout-lined will block out the light for a good night's sleep. This look is very simple, and the panels will frame the window or door openings nicely when pulled back during the day.

Another option is to layer the window treatments in the same manner that you dress a bed by using a combination of sheers and opaque draperies. The sheer fabric works during the day to diffuse the light coming in, and at night the opaque panels can be drawn to keep light out. It's a double treatment, which can look very elegant in a bedroom.

A combination of blinds or shades or plantation shutters also works nicely when framed by curtain panels to add dimension to a bedroom window. The panels can be solid, have a subtle pattern, or trim or banding in an accent color that complements the color scheme and bedding; but whatever you do, please don't ever buy curtains or valances that are the exact match to the print of your comforter set. I know they sell them and you might be tempted, but I personally feel this a big no-no because it's a dated look—similar to scarves and valances.

Design Your Life

In a bedroom suite, the sensory experience can be enhanced to create the right atmosphere for sleeping, relaxation and romance. Scented candles, diffusers, linen sprays and incense can affect the psychological and physical well-being of a person, which is the reason I love to use these details in my room makeovers. You can choose a different scent for your bedroom depending on what time of the day it is and what you're trying to accomplish. For example, in the evening, lavender, sandalwood or sage are all scents that have relaxing properties and will help you sleep better. In the morning, citrus, mint and pine aromas are invigorating and help you start your day. Of course, since the bedroom is also a place for romance, fill the air with the scent of fruits and flowers such as jasmine or gardenia, which awakens passion. Perfumed sachets placed in your closet and drawers will also give your clothes a fresh and clean smell. These are small indulgences that will make you feel extra special every night and turn your bedroom into a retreat.

Before

Doors as Headboards

This bedroom lacks a focal point. It has only a mattress, which doesn't feel very inviting. When the budget is tight, we have to get the most creative. Let's make a unique headboard for this room by shopping at a home improvement store for this easy and fun project.

A bedroom without a headboard lacks a focal point. Yes, a mattress is functional for sleeping, but it's not exactly making a design statement in the room. Depending on the size and style of bed that you like, buying a bed frame directly at a furniture store can exceed your decorating budget. Here's how to get the look for less by shopping at your nearest home improvement store. Hollow-core interior doors make great headboards! The panel style works well in a rustic or traditional setting, whereas a smooth front has a modern look because of the simple lines.

The standard door height is 80 inches (203 cm), and when installed on the wall horizontally, the width can accommodate a king-size bed, so it's a perfect fit. For smaller mattress sizes, you can install them vertically to achieve the same effect and shorten the width. They are available primed or in a natural finish, so you can choose to stain them to bring out the wood grain or paint them an accent color as in this makeover to make the headboard really pop. Stack a few to create more height or place side by side to create width. In this bedroom makeover, I stacked two doors painted in gray and illuminated the headboard from the back with LED lights. Another option is to hang frames as artwork right on them. The frames can be highlighted with a picture light, which casts a nice glow over the bed. Simple, stylish and modern—best of all, it is DIY friendly.

Materials

Hollow-core doors—style and quantity of your choice

Paint—color of your choice or stain

Paint tray, foam roller, paint brush

Sandpaper (optional)

Cordless drill

1" x 2" (2.5 x 5-cm) pine

Miter box and saw (optional)

1⅝" (4-cm) screws

French cleat picture hanger kits—200 lb (91 kg) weight

Measuring tape

Level

LED ribbon light kit (optional)

Hammer

Steps

1. Begin by purchasing door(s) at a home improvement store and select the style you like most—panel or smooth front. Depending on the width you select, the more you stack, the more dramatic the headboard will be. I stacked two 28-inch (71-cm) width doors, but if you prefer a minimalist and modern style, one door will work, too.

If you're buying them in natural wood, choose your favorite stain or paint. If you buy them primed, you can proceed to paint them in your favorite color. I painted mine in gray and used the paint brush to cut in around all the recessed panels, and switched to the foam roller for the even surfaces. Once the paint is dry, I used a sanding block to distress the finish, which adds more character so it doesn't look brand new.

2. Stack two doors horizontally to achieve this same look. To secure them together, use the drill to attach 1 x 2-inch (2.5 x 5-cm) pine on the back across the top and sides, leaving a 2-inch (5-cm) space from the edge. This means the wood on the sides is cut down to 54 inches (137 cm), which is 2 inches (5 cm) less than the height of the two doors stacked. Cut the wood across the top down to 73 inches (185 cm) to fit in between the two side pieces. You can easily cut this on your own using a miter box and saw, or your local home improvement store can cut it for you if you give them the measurements. Attach all the wood pieces to the door using the 1⅝-inch (4-cm) screws.

3. To prepare the doors to hang, install the mounting brackets 12 inches (30 cm) from the edge of the 1 x 2-inch (2.5 x 5-cm) wood on either side. The French cleat bracket is 18 inches (46 cm); so by installing two, the weight of the headboard will be evenly distributed on the wall.

4. The DIY headboard should be centered on the wall, and the bottom should be flush with the top of the mattress. Begin by marking your center point.

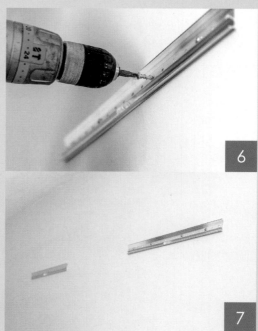

5. Measure the height of the mattress from the floor. Add this number to the length of the stacked doors and transfer measurement to the wall where it meets the center mark. This is where the top of the headboard will be on the wall.

6. Measure 2 inches (5 cm) down from that mark and draw a line using a level across the wall almost as wide as your new headboard. This correlates to the placement of the wall tracks that interlock with the mounting brackets on the back of the headboard. When hung, the headboard will be the correct height.

7. Transfer the same measurements for the brackets on the back of the headboard to the wall, which are 8 inches (20 cm) out from the center mark, and secure the wall tracks using the bubble level included. Make sure you use the proper wall anchors if you don't hit a stud.

8. Your new headboard is now ready to be hung, or you can take it a step further by adding LED ribbon light on the back to illuminate the headboard from behind for a cool effect at night. Attach the LED along the 2-inch (5-cm) border with the clips that came in packaging using a hammer. I connected two lights to go around the entire perimeter and gathered any extra with a cable tie.

After

Total cost for this project averages $100 to $200, which is less expensive than buying a traditional headboard. Now you have a custom piece that makes a statement in any bedroom.

Before

CHAPTER 4

Dining Rooms
Design a Style Menu for Entertaining in a Beautiful Setting

As a kid, a dining table was just a place to eat. Now, as an adult, I view this space so differently. A dining room is where memories are made, traditions are celebrated and where you spend time with those you love the most—friends and family—gathered around the dinner table sharing stories and, yes, of course, indulging in gastronomical delights (just a fancy way of saying "delicious food"). If the kitchen is the heart of the home, I would say a dining room is a close second. It makes sense, since after you cook you need a place to eat, right? They go hand in hand.

As a designer, the setting you create is just as important as what is on the menu. It's an opportunity to create an unforgettable experience as you decorate this room in your home because you know it has the potential to leave a lasting impression. I'm not only referring to guests when you host your next dinner party; your entire family, and especially the children, will have fond memories in this room, where so many special moments in their lives were celebrated—everything from birthdays to holidays and more.

There are three items in a dining room that make all the difference in the design. Can you guess what they are? Two might come to mind as obvious choices: the dining table and chairs. Yet, there is still a third element, which enhances the ambience for dining and entertaining, and that is the light fixture. I cannot tell you how many times I've seen the wrong fixture above a dining table. What could've been a wow moment turns lackluster at first sight. In other rooms, the lighting might not have such a starring role, but in a dining room it can make or break the design.

1 Walls

Are you looking for ideas to refresh the look of your dining room? You might have a nice dining set, but the space is missing a wow factor. Well, a feature wall can definitely make a design statement. It doesn't take much to create a focal point on one wall, and it can make all the difference.

The trend in today's modern and new construction homes is to have an open floor plan. In this case, dining room walls might be shared with other adjacent rooms. In most traditional or older homes, the dining space is usually a completely separate room. The same design ideas can apply to both; however, it can be more challenging in the former as whatever you do on any specific wall in the dining room has to take into account the other areas that are also visible. That being said, it's still doable; with different wall treatments you can help define the dining room area from the rest of the home.

Paint

Depending on how many walls surround the dining room, paint is always the most economical way to set the tone. Generally speaking, the darker the color, the more intimate it will be and the bolder the color, the more dramatic it will look. This all relates back to the decorating style and color scheme you have in other areas of the home, since the rooms should have a natural flow from one to another as part of an open concept. In other words, if your dining room is open to the living room and kitchen where you have warm neutrals such as gray and taupe, adding a bright red on the walls in the dining area might not be the best choice. It's a complete juxtaposition. And vice versa, if you have an eclectic personality and have fun and bright colors throughout, but your dining room is a stark white, then it falls flat. It's as if two different people live in the home, so you need to be conscious of this.

It's certainly okay to keep the same wall color in the dining room as you have in other areas. However, if you still wish to create a focal point, painting an accent wall is a great option. The inspiration for the color can come from the chair fabric, an area rug, wall art or an adjacent space open to the dining room that you wish to contrast or complement as part of your home's color palette.

Ceilings

Most dining room ceilings are white, but why choose what everyone else has? When a ceiling is painted a complementary color, it can become a dramatic focal point in the room to frame the light fixture. Ideally, for this to work the dining area needs to be in a separate room and not have a ceiling that is shared by other adjacent rooms. If that's the case, be daring and consider doing this—especially if you have crown molding or a tray ceiling, which features a center section that is several inches (or several feet) higher than the areas around the perimeter of the room. You have a few ways to do this: (1) Paint the tray ceiling portion the same color as the walls, (2) paint it a deeper version of your wall color or (3) paint it a lighter version of your wall color. When exploring these options, consider the height of your room and the natural light coming in. If your ceiling is tall, darker colors will create a more intimate setting; lighter colors can create the illusion of more space, making the room appear taller.

Before

The metallic wallpaper on one wall was the perfect backdrop to define the dining room in this apartment.

Wood trim adds architectural detail to an otherwise plain wall. It creates a lot of visual impact without spending too much on materials.

Wallpaper

The goal with an accent wall is to make a statement, and wallpaper is another natural choice for a dining room. It's available in a multitude of colors, patterns and textures that can even resemble popular decorative paint finishes like linen, suede or metallic. It can look formal or whimsical in your dining space regardless of whether it covers an entire room or just a feature wall. The specific pattern is subjective to your liking and style, but large-scale wallpaper definitely makes a bigger impact than a small one. Wallpaper can be used as another layering element in the dining room décor creating visual interest, but be careful not to overwhelm the room with too many busy patterns—mainly if you plan to hang artwork on the walls or have a print on the window treatments or fabric on chairs. If you like the look but are still afraid to commit to an entire wall, consider using wallpaper above a chair rail or inside panel molding for a more subtle effect. Wallpaper has made a comeback and is great way to add elegance and ambience, turning an otherwise plain wall into a design feature.

Trim Molding

Whether the dining room is part of an open floor plan or is its own separate room, trim molding is also an inexpensive way to add high impact in formal areas. This architectural detail can work in every décor style, from traditional to modern, to create a feature wall or around the entire room. A traditional application might be partway up a wall as a chair rail or wainscoting, but it can look just as modern when you cover an entire surface with a three-dimensional grid pattern. By installing the wood trim directly on the wall, it mimics the look of paneling when it's all painted the same color, which is what I recommend. In this small dining room, I used lattice strips to create a focal wall, and even though it's painted a classic white the textural element is what grabs your attention and defines this space. Wood is the most popular trim option because it's available in a variety of sizes and it's easy to stain or paint and install; but you can find other alternatives that resemble wood, which are more resistant to moisture and are less expensive. I really love how this wall treatment transformed this small dining room.

2 Furniture

A formal dining room might not be used on a daily basis since breakfast nooks or kitchen islands tend to become the main gathering hub for families, but the furnishings still play an important role. It's similar to a living room. Although you have one, the family gravitates to a family room or den, right? In the meantime, both spaces have to make their own style statement as part of the overall look of the home while it's not being used and be ready to meet the needs of the family when entertaining guests.

First, and foremost, the dining room has to be functional. It's easy to go into a furniture store and pick out a set, but similar to any other room in the house, you can still create a custom look by mixing pieces from different collections. This really will depend, once again, on your decorating style.

There is nothing wrong with buying a dining set that typically brings a table and four chairs and, of course, if you need more chairs, buy more of the same. It does take the guesswork out for many homeowners, and I can understand its appeal. It can actually work well in a modern setting to maintain clean lines and a cohesive look. However, if you're influenced by other eclectic styles such as farmhouse, coastal, global, vintage and more, then you can personalize the set a lot more by mixing pieces. In our inspiration room, the style was rustic, yet refined. The table has a subtle washed patina and features turned legs and a trestle base, which contrasts beautifully with the luxe design of the dining chairs in soft, cream velvet with button diamond tufting. The shimmer of the fabrics gives a hint of glam. At the furniture showroom I was pulling chairs from one set and bringing them over to the other to show the homeowner a custom grouping, so don't be afraid to ask for assistance to do the same when shopping.

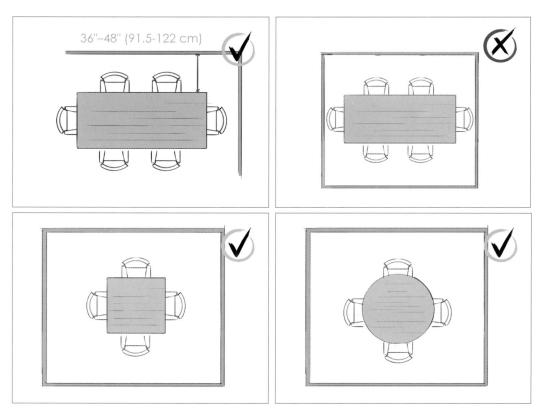

The table should mimic the shape of the dining room floor plan for visual harmony. Perfectly square rooms look and function best with a square or round table for better flow around the space.

Table Shape & Size

The first thing to consider is the size of the table. You have to make sure it fits in your space with enough room to comfortably sit and walk around it. A good rule of thumb is to leave between 36 and 48 inches (91.5 and 122 cm) of clearance from the table to the wall or any piece of furniture you might have in the room, such as a server or china hutch. It's important to take into account the table leaves as well. As you're shopping, take measurements of the table and create an outline on the floor of your dining room with painter's tape so you can visualize it better in your space.

Before

There are many shapes and sizes out there, and the dimensions of the room will determine which one is better suited for your home. Round and square tables work best in square rooms or small spaces. Personally, my favorite is using a round table because it is a nice juxtaposition within the box shape of a room. Trust me on this. In tight spaces, another designer trick is to choose a glass table top to make the room appear more spacious. There are many circumference sizes available, so this will depend on how many seats you can fit based on the calculations of the room. Consider that each person will need about 2 feet (61 cm) of legroom around the table. You have to be realistic about this to avoid overcrowding the room with too many chairs or else your guests will end up touching elbows. The maximum seating you can probably get out of a round or square table is probably eight.

Most homes will be able to accommodate a rectangular table at least 36 inches (91.5 cm) wide, so there is ample space for place settings and food dishes. In terms of the length and how many chairs it can fit, it has to be proportional to your room's dimensions. Many manufacturers offer removable extensions to make the table longer and accommodate additional seating for special occasions. My advice is to pay attention to the table base at the showroom, so an extra chair doesn't fall right in front of a leg. We've all been there trying to squeeze around a dinner table and end up banging our knee against the base. Ouch. As host or hostess, you have to keep this in mind to make sure your guests can sit comfortably at a large dinner party. Even if you're a family of four, I recommend buying a table for at least six (if you have the space) because you know you're going to need it when guests come over. Normally, as the table length increases, the width will increase, so this also affects your calculations.

Table Seating

It all comes together with the dining chairs, and this is where you can be as unique as your personality. The trend is to mix different styles of chairs and seating around the table, but this is really a matter of preference. I know I keep saying this, but at the end of the day, it's your home and it needs to look how you like it since you'll be the one living in it. Regardless of whether you wish to take a risk and mix it up or keep them all the same, buying new chairs is an easy way to update the look of your dining room on a budget.

Traditional seating combines armchairs at the head of the table with side chairs. This is a classic look we've always seen, whereby all the chairs typically match the finish of the table and the only difference is two chairs have arms. Why be ordinary when you can be extraordinary?! I say this is the perfect opportunity to add drama and be the host and hostess with the "mostest."

Host & Hostess Chair

Switching up the host and hostess chair to a different style is the way to go. The trick is to keep the scale in proportion or slightly taller than the side chairs for it to be effective. You find this option with many dining sets at furniture stores because manufacturers realize that the consumer is now looking for the ability to customize their dining room. I especially like doing this when a dining set has matching wood tables and chairs. By adding an upholstered host and hostess chair it helps to break up all the hard surfaces next to each other. The fabric color and/or finish can also be different. Often times, you can repurpose dining chairs as accent chairs in a living room, too. Rules are meant to be broken, and even outdoor furniture can be used as indoor seating around a table. In one makeover I used all-weather wicker wingback chairs at the head of the table to create a casual dining room with farmhouse charm. This is what great design is all about—doing something unexpected.

Benches

Another popular seating combination we see at dining tables is adding benches. The material of the bench will determine how casual or formal it will look. For example, wood and metal benches lend themselves to farmhouse and industrial styles; yet an upholstered piece can be used in a more elegant setting, like the inspiration room where the velvet fabric adds a touch of luxury. It can seat three guests, so instead of buying three chairs at a higher price, you get the same amount of seating for less. Without a back or arms, benches tuck in nicely underneath the table, so it's also a good option for smaller spaces to keep the dining room feeling open. I'm a big fan of this look.

Don't be afraid to combine all three trends: host/hostess chairs with side chairs and benches. For this eclectic grouping to work, though, keep the same fabric and style consistent with two of the seating options for visual harmony.

Servers & Storage

China hutches date back to the seventeenth century when craftsmen built these special cabinets for the wealthy to display their fine china and porcelain. To this day, they are still sold as part of any dining room collection. Although the look is very traditional, the idea has evolved into more contemporary and less-bulky servers. Other terms used to describe this piece are sideboards or buffets.

The square footage of the dining room will determine whether you can accommodate more furniture in the space, but I'm a huge fan of servers because they create a focal point on one wall. Since most dining tables float in the center of the room, a server is both decorative and functional to help anchor the space. Inside you can store serving platters, dinnerware, linens and glasses; the top can be used for food dishes while entertaining buffet style. It's a versatile piece that can also be used as a bar and media console in your living or family room. I mention this because recycling furniture from one room to another is a great way to update spaces on a budget.

In the inspiration room, I chose an ivory color to contrast against the wood table. It creates its own statement and defines the dining room wall in this open floor plan. The dishes are visible through the glass-front doors, so they become part of the décor. The size of the server is 86 inches (218.5 cm) wide, so it's in proportion with the width of the wall. This is important because on a large wall a smaller piece will look odd and vice versa. Servers are also great to place additional light sources such as beautiful lamps and other decorative accessories.

If you like the idea of a server but find you don't have enough room for a traditional piece, a console table is a good option. The depth is usually between 12 and 15 inches (30.5 and 38 cm), so they work well in tight spaces and you can still decorate the top. I used a two-tone wood piece with elegantly carved legs in a bay window in one dining room makeover. It has the look of an antique farmhouse, which complemented the more refined style of the dining table and chairs the homeowner already had.

Before

Instead of, or in addition to, a server if you happen to have a large dining room with tall ceilings, curio cabinets also make a beautiful backdrop. The vertical height makes the room more intimate and you can still display your china or collectibles. In a rustic farmhouse style, look for curio cabinets that have beautifully paneled doors with glass panes and are topped by crown molding. They can be painted or natural wood. The latched hardware is also a nice detail for authentic appeal. In a modern setting, look for clean lines, metal finishes and sliding glass doors and shelves. You can place two side by side to make a bold statement in your dining room.

3 Accessories

Truth be known, compared to other rooms in the home, a dining room doesn't require a lot of accessorizing. However, it does need the correct amount and in the right place to make it a warm and inviting space to gather and entertain. Without the accessories, well, a dining room is just a functional space with a table and chairs for eating; I can't even refer to it as dining. The reason we go out to eat at restaurants (fast-food excluded), especially fine dining, is truly for the ambience. It's a combination of the food, service and atmosphere that creates a comfortable dining experience. Have you noticed that the lighting is usually always dim? It's no coincidence that restaurants do this. Low light creates a more relaxing and intimate space.

This is where we tackle the third design element a dining room must absolutely have to rise above the rest—pun intended—and I'm referring to the ceiling light fixture.

Lighting

The overhead fixture defines a dining room. It's not only a necessity for general lighting when dining, but it's also a design feature that has to be harmonious with the scale of the table and the ceiling height. My preference is to always install a hanging pendant or chandelier because it helps to visually fill the empty area between the table and ceiling—otherwise the room looks bare.

In many cases, I've seen a ceiling fan installed over a dining table, and it's a big pet peeve of mine that doesn't make sense. A ceiling fan is never practical to have turned on while you're eating because the draft will make the food cold and it can create a mess with burning candles dripping wax all over the table. So why have one in a dining room? Yep, a big no-no.

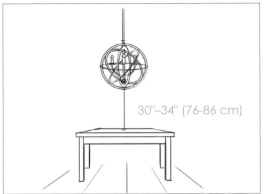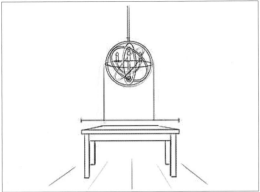

30"–34" (76-86 cm)

A light fixture is a decorative and functional element that defines a dining room. It should relate and balance the scale of the table underneath, so proper install height and size needs to be considered.

Other scenarios include a light fixture that is completely the wrong style or hung too high. In the photo on page 106 you can see how the contemporary light fixture didn't relate to the table underneath because it was installed too high. The shape was also too small for the size of the room and table length. Although the homeowner had a beautiful dining set, the visual weight between table and fixture was not in balance. When compared to the new fixture, you can see how one change made a world of difference in this dining room. It's a 26-inch (66-cm) wide orb chandelier that combines weathered oak wood with antique forged iron, so it's the perfect marriage of styles to complement the table—a match made in heaven. This demonstrates how important a light fixture is as a design element in a dining room. It's like finding the right blouse to the skirt, or the right shirt to the pants.

Light Fixture Size

The question most homeowners have is what size fixture will work? Here is a formula used in the industry. To determine the height of the chandelier, multiply your ceiling height by 2.5 or 3 to get the recommended measurement in inches. For example, a standard 8-foot (2.5-m) ceiling would call for a chandelier height of 20 to 24 inches (51 to 61 cm).

To determine the diameter above a dining table, it should be two-thirds to three-quarters the size of the table width. If the light fixture extends past the width of the table it will not only overpower the room, but guests may bump into it when getting up; too small and it will look odd and out of scale, too. It's a yin and yang effect you wish to achieve.

Once you find the perfect size, the length you choose to hang the chandelier over the table will also impact the overall look. Of course, there's a formula for that, too.

The right chandelier can make a style statement on its own in a dining room. Modern farmhouse and industrial trends are reflected in fixtures with an iron finish and exposed bulbs, whereas crystals are a classic and elegant look.

On average, hang your fixture approximately 30 to 34 inches (76 to 86.5 cm) over a table with an 8-foot (2.5-m) ceiling height to keep sight lines open; however, if your ceilings are higher than 8 feet (244 cm), mount the chandelier an additional 3 inches (7.5 cm) higher for each foot of ceiling. All of this is like taking a crash course in mathematics, but I promise it's easier than it sounds.

Light Fixture Styles

Oh, my goodness. If the measurements weren't enough, choosing a style for the light fixture can also be tricky. This is really a matter of preference inspired by your decorating style. I know I keep repeating this, but it's so true. You can never go wrong with traditional chandeliers; but pendant lighting can also make a dramatic impact in your dining room and work in a range of styles from modern to farmhouse to industrial.

Grouping three or more together is most effective over your table, but lighting manufacturers have made it easy by offering multi-pendants within the same fixture. Multi-light configurations have a larger canopy, which is the lamp part used to cover the ceiling electrical box, and I bring this up because it should be proportional to the size of the table. Choose a rectangular canopy for rectangular tables and a round canopy over round or square dining tables. It's a small detail, but once it's installed you'll see how mimicking the shape makes sense for visual consistency.

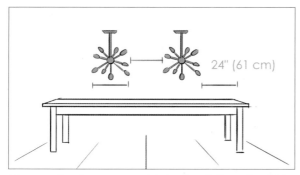

24" (61 cm)

The spacing between multiple chandeliers should be even for the fixtures to look balanced hanging over the length of the table.

Another popular choice is drum pendants, available in many sizes from medium to large. They make a bold statement with their simple design and look better when placed above a round or square table. You can find them in many materials, from pleated fabric to frosted glass to laser-cut metal and are often finished with a bottom diffuser to minimize glare. Some styles even offer mini-crystal chandeliers in the center—modern glam all in one.

Hanging multiple chandeliers or pendants above a long table is a popular design trend in lighting. I keep emphasizing that the size of the table always needs to be taken into consideration for any light fixture to work, but even more so with pendants. They are minimalist designs, so for any table more than 72 inches (183 cm) long, I recommend two to create a balanced look and provide adequate lighting across the table. Doing so will require a second ceiling box installed by a professional electrician. For longer tables, a third ceiling box should be considered, too. This does change the scale of the fixtures that work best in the space, so there is a formula for that, too.

When hanging two or more chandeliers over a table, divide the table length by the number of chandeliers plus one. This will give you an approximate diameter for each chandelier and the spacing between each one. For example, to hang two chandeliers over a table that is 72 inches (183 cm) long (72 divided by 2 + 1) = 24 inches (61 cm) for the width of each chandelier, and they should be hung 24 inches from each end of the table. Let's do one more calculation for hanging three chandeliers over a table that is 72 inches (183 cm) long (72 divide by 3 + 1) = 18 inches (45.5 cm) for the width of each chandelier, and they should be hung 18 inches (45.5 cm) from each end of the table and between each one.

Dimmer Switches

Dimmer switches are a decorating secret to change the mood of a room with just a touch. I love having the ability to dim the lights in a dining room—especially when you're enjoying the romantic glow of candles as a table centerpiece. Controlling the intensity of the overhead lighting can make the room feel more intimate and provide excellent ambiance for a dinner party or gathering.

Table Lamps

In addition to the ambient lighting from the ceiling fixture, I like to add accent lighting in the form of table lamps on a server. There are specific lamp styles known as "buffet lamps," which usually are 32 to 36 inches (81 to 91.5 cm) tall with a thin base, sometimes referred to as console lamps or candlestick lamps; but smaller table lamps can work in a dining room setting, too. They simply look great flanking a mirror over a server, which is how I use them in dining rooms. It's another way of layering lighting to dress up a room.

Area Rug

To add an area rug or not is a big debate in dining rooms. The hesitation I hear from many homeowners is that it will stain easily underneath a dining table. It's a valid point. Here's what I think: in an open floor plan dining rooms don't require area rugs as long as there is one in the adjacent room, which is typically a living or family room. There should be an area rug in that room already to define the grouping. Therefore, you don't need to add another one in a nearby space. If you want to, that's totally fine, but it's not absolutely necessary. However, if the dining room is a completely separate room, then I do feel an area rug is a nice touch to add warmth in the space.

The smallest area rug you should consider for a dining room is probably an 8 x 10-foot (2.5 x 3-m) size to accommodate all the legs of the chairs for a standard table that seats four to six people. For more precise measurements, add 24 to 30 inches (61 to 76 cm) around all sides of the table to allow room for the chairs to easily slide in and out. Ideally, the rug should not end up underneath any additional piece of furniture you have in the space, such as a server or china hutch. This is important because an area rug looks nicer when you leave at least 18 inches (45.5 cm) of flooring uncovered around the perimeter of the room.

The same principles of design that we covered in the Living Rooms chapter (page 60) apply here, too. Choose a rug shape that complements the size of the room and the table. Your only choice for a rectangular table is a rectangular area rug and a square table looks best with a square rug; with a round table, you can consider a round area rug or a square one. The latter is the only table that can work with both area rug shapes.

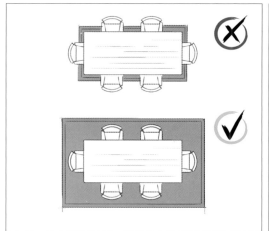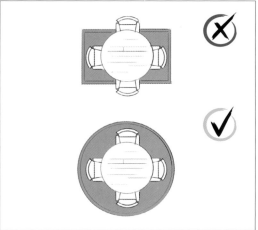

Area rugs should be bigger than the size of the dining table and chairs. Match the shape of the rug with the style of the table for a harmonious space.

An affordable way to create a custom size for a longer table is to place two solid area rugs side by side. This will increase the length without adding width and because you're not matching a pattern, you won't have a visible seam. Look for flat weave, short-pile rugs or synthetics for durability and easy cleanup. There is a wide selection of all-weather area rugs in trendy patterns that look great inside. These indoor/outdoor rugs are perfect for playrooms and high-traffic areas, too.

Area rugs can be as fashionable and as subtle as you wish depending on the color and pattern. In a dining room, they can also be used as the inspiration behind the color scheme. When deciding on a design, think of the tips I shared in the Living Rooms chapter (page 63) on mixing and matching the scale of patterns, solids and/or stripes on throw pillows. It's the same concept to create a unifying color story throughout all the elements and pull different hues from the rug as accent colors throughout the room—wall paint, artwork, upholstery on chairs or window panels.

Multicolor and bold patterned rugs have the advantage of disguising spills, but it will become a focal point, so you need to make sure it doesn't compete with anything else in the room; stripes make the room look wider or longer, while plain-colored rugs with interesting textures or geometric patterns work better in a modern setting. The most important thing is you want the rug to complement the furniture style and add more visual interest in the dining room.

Mirrors

When it works, it works. Placing a mirror over a server in a dining room is a classic look that works well in every decorating style. It's a beautiful accent that usually becomes a secondary focal point when you walk into the space—in addition to the dining set. Mirrors can reflect light and can make the room feel larger. You can choose a frame style and color that coordinates with your dining furniture or you can have it make a bold statement with a unique frame that complements existing design elements—similar to wall art.

The key is to find the right size that will hang above the server. A good rule of thumb is the mirror should be two-thirds or three-quarters the width of the furniture to create visual balance; however, feel free to go wider, up to the width of the furniture, if it works in your space. For an eclectic look, you can also group a collection of mirrors on the wall to occupy the same width above the server. Rectangular or square mirrors are the most popular because they mimic the shape of the rest of the furniture in the room; but I'm also a fan of round mirrors to juxtapose all the straight lines and complement a round table, for example. The shape doesn't really matter as long as you like it and you take into account the measurements to ensure it's the proper scale for the room.

Mirrors over servers are a great focal point in a dining room, especially when framed with beautiful lamps. It should not exceed the width of the server and an ideal height is about 6-9" (15-23 cm) from the top of the furniture.

Over a server, it's best to hang the mirror leaving a space of 6 to 9 inches (15 to 23 cm) between the bottom of the frame and the top of the server. This creates a nice grouping. The height of the ceiling is only a determining factor when it comes to the orientation: horizontal or vertical. Horizontal always works, but if you have vaulted, loft-style or 10-foot (3-m) ceilings and higher, tall mirrors can fill the expansive area, creating a more intimate space. This direction also works when you lean the mirror against the wall on the server—instead of hanging it. It has a more modern aesthetic. Be aware that mirrors in a dining room act as wall art, so whatever is reflected becomes a part of the decor.

Centerpieces

Centerpieces refer to table décor when the dining room is not being used. Often times leaving the surface bare can make the entire room feel incomplete. The go-to accessory is usually a vase with flowers, but it might not be practical as everyday décor. The second go-to item is a candleholder. I love using them, but that alone on the table won't necessarily do the trick. To give it more presence, I like repeating the candleholders (maximum three), evenly spaced along the length of the table. They can all be the same style and height for uniformity; however, you can also make the center one taller and then flank the sides with a smaller version for a sense of unified variety: simple, modern and beautiful. Depending on your style, you can use mason jars for a touch of rustic charm; or metal lanterns or hurricane glass candleholders. They all work. You can even use these vessels as decorative planters by adding succulents, pebble rocks and moss. A touch of greenery is always nice to add another layer of interest on the table.

Equally as impactful is creating a cluster of different items on the table top. This goes back to the principles of creating a tablescape and/or vignette. The center of the table is the focal point, so this is where I begin by grouping different objects, including a decorative tray and a geometric candleholder, and then proceed to balance the arrangement with other unexpected accessories on the side.

Two things to consider: You want the table to breathe visually, so don't overcrowd the top with bulky items, and don't make them too tall whereby they are too close to the bottom of the chandelier. Of course, this will depend on your ceiling height, but you certainly want to leave adequate space—2 feet (61 cm)—between the two, so that each design element can have its own starring moment in the room.

Window Treatments

Window treatments are important to enhance the overall environment, and I tend to keep them fairly simple in a dining room setting since I want the focus to be on the dining table. In a casual setting I gravitate to light and airy fabrics such as sheers to create a softer backdrop, especially if privacy is not a concern. In a formal look, you can use heavier fabrics with sheen and woven textiles. Both styles will work better when you install them from ceiling to floor—even though your window might be shorter. Don't be afraid to hang the curtain rod higher than the top of the window frame because this is a great trick designer's use to make a room appear taller.

Design Your Life

In a dining room, candles are often used as part of the centerpiece on the table and remain décor unless we have a dinner party. Similar to using the fine china, most of us are programmed to only light candles on special occasions when guests come over. I say why wait? Live the present. I didn't grow up lighting candles when we ate dinner every day either, but I did notice how different the experience was when we did during a celebration or holiday get-together. There's something about the soft glow of a candle that makes everything more enjoyable and intimate.

Candles seem to have an hourglass effect when lit at dinner; it's as if time moves slower and you feel more at peace. I know it's something so simple to point out, but try it. The next time you sit down for dinner—whether it's only you, a party of two or the entire family—give yourself permission to light a candleholder on any ordinary day. Even a small votive. You'll see and experience how different the mood will be around the table. Don't wait for that special occasion. Light the candles, use the fine china . . . I know it's a cliché, but there is no time like the present to enjoy life. Sometimes we all need subtle reminders to do that.

Before

Rustic Wood Mirror

Are you ready to create a one-of-a-kind mirror that will look a lot more expensive than it was to make? This is my kind of project! A door mirror is functional, but with a few materials we can transform it to make a major impact in the décor of the room.

Mirrors are used in design to create the illusion of more space in a room. They reflect natural light and can highlight beautiful details, such as a chandelier in a dining room, by reflecting them into your vision from different angles. Mirrors are also considered statement pieces because they become the art in any room and on any wall. Instead of a painting or artwork, an ornate or textured frame is just as effective to enhance the décor.

Of course, the bigger the mirror, the more expensive they are. With rustic finishes and the farmhouse style being ever so popular, I decided to make my own DIY version out of a door mirror. This long rectangular mirror comes with a simple, plastic frame. The price is good, but the style factor is lackluster. But it's nothing a trip to my local home improvement store can't fix by shopping in the lumber section for some basic supplies.

Materials

1" x 8" (2.5 x 20.5-cm) pine

Measuring tape

Wood stain—weathered gray

Staining pads

Disposable gloves

Cordless drill

10" (25.5-cm) mending plates

⅝" (1.5-cm) wood screws

Frameless door mirror—16" x 60" (40.5 x 152.5 cm)

Mirror clips—comes with door mirror

½" (1.5-cm) sheet metal screws

French cleat picture hanger kit—300 lb (136 kg) weight

Level

Polyurethane (optional)

Steps

1. The idea is to use the 1 x 8-inch (2.5 x 20.5-cm) wood planks to frame the mirror. Begin by measuring and cutting the two longest sides 1 inch (2.5 cm) less than the height of the door mirror. In this project it was 59 inches (150 cm). This is to overlap the frame by ½ inch (1.5 cm) all around, so we can secure the mirror from behind. Your local home improvement store can cut the wood for you as long as you give them the exact measurements.

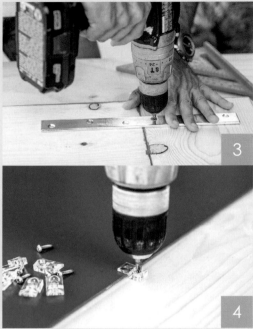

2. Cut the two shortest sides to 29½ inches (75 cm). This takes into account the width of the mirror at 16 inches (40.5 cm) plus the wood we cut in Step 1 that will frame the top and bottom at 7¼ inches (18.5 cm) each plank, which equals 14½ inches (37 cm). Total combined width is 30½ inches minus 1 inch equals 29½ inches (75 cm). This allows a ½ inch (1.5 cm) overlap all around to secure the mirror from behind.

Apply the weathered gray stain with the staining pads and use disposable gloves to protect your hands. The more coats, the darker the stain. Once it is dry, you can give it a finish coat with a polyurethane, which makes it more durable. However, since the mirror will be installed indoors, it is not necessary on this project. I also prefer the matte finish of the stain, which looks more rustic.

3. To build the frame, turn it upside down and use the drill to secure the pieces with the 10-inch (25.5-cm) mending plates across the top and bottom using ⅝-inch (1.5-cm) wood screws. If the screws are too long they will damage the front of the frame.

4. Secure the door mirror to the back of the frame using the mirror clips that came in the packaging. I used ½-inch (1.5-cm) sheet metal screws because the original screws were too long and would've damaged the front of the frame.

5. Attach the mounting bracket from the French cleat kit in the top center of the mirror frame.

6. Measure the center of the wall and secure the interlocking track using the bubble level included at the height you wish to hang the mirror.

After

No one will guess this began as a frameless door mirror. It looks expensive and substantial without the high price tag. The rustic wood frame can also complement many decorating styles, from global to farmhouse.

Before

JAXSON

CHAPTER 5

Nurseries
Room to Grow While Saving Money in the Piggy Bank

Designing a dream nursery space is a special moment in the lives of soon-to-be parents. The expectations to make everything perfect for the arrival of the baby can sometimes be a daunting task—after all, this is the environment the new addition to the family will be calling home. Every parent wishes for their nursery to be whimsical, beautiful, playful, imaginative and charming—all these adjectives and more.

What first-time parents don't realize is that the nursery phase of the décor can be very short, so the original design needs to have more longevity or else you might find yourself updating the room again in about a year. During the first months at home, a baby usually sleeps in a bassinette in the parent's bedroom to be close for monitoring. Therefore, the nursery might only be used for feeding, napping and changing diapers. By the time your child can fully transition into the nursery on its own, he or she might be closer to becoming a toddler.

Keep in mind this timeline if you wish for the room to grow with your baby well beyond his or her nursery years to save money. In my experience, there are two things that can limit the potential growth of the design in a nursery: décor that is excessively baby themed and buying too much baby furniture. I'm referring to decorating themes that might be taken overboard with an explosion of matching accessories; consequently, when furniture shopping for a nursery, the rule of thumb is less is more. Many first-time parents feel compelled to buy all the matching pieces to the collection, which might overcrowd the room. More details ahead on this topic.

Before

1 Walls

As you stare at the walls in the nursery, visualize first where the crib will go. It's best when it's placed in front of the most expansive wall in the space that has no window. This will determine the focal point that you can play up in the design and give you a footprint to lay out the rest of the furnishings in the room.

Painting the nursery is usually the step that sets the decorating process in motion, and the first decision to be made is coming up with a color scheme. Although there are many colors to choose from, we all know the two most popular are blue for boys and pink for girls. There is nothing wrong with this if that's what you like, but I also suggest looking for inspiration in other colors found in the crib bedding you chose to break from the norm. If you want the paint color to work throughout different stages from infancy to toddler, stay away from pastels and primary hues. They have a tendency to look, well, baby-ish by the time your child is older. Instead, chose deeper shades, which have more gray in the paint mix and look modern and classic. Soothing shades of sky blue, sea foam green, dusty pinks, soft whites and grays are proven nursery colors that evoke feelings of serenity and peace and have a calming effect on the baby. You can go bolder, but pay attention to the natural light coming into the room. If the nursery is on the smaller side you can paint an accent wall in a darker shade, but leave the rest of the walls in a lighter tone so it doesn't close in the walls.

Safety should always be the number one priority in a baby's room, and you might want to choose paint that is eco-friendly in this stage of decorating as well. Most of the paint brands offer a product in their line that is water-based and eliminates the VOCs (volatile organic compounds), which can have an impact on the indoor air quality. All parents want to create a clean and safe environment for their little one, and there are paints that are safer with natural pigments and no odors. This is really a matter of preference, similar to choosing organic baby products, but at least you know you have options.

In our inspiration makeover for a boy's nursery, the base color chosen was once again a gray palette. As I keep saying throughout the book, it is the new neutral in home décor and, hey, when it works, it works. What's nice about gray is it is very gender fluid and can be used in both a boy and girl nursery. Gray is the dominating color found in the whimsical bedding featuring jungle animals. However, we also took the inspiration one step further and used paint to create a custom mural for the wall behind the crib. It became the focal point of the nursery. The design was inspired from a decorative frame the soon-to-be mommy had purchased, and we kept the color scheme monochromatic—meaning we used different tones of the same color. By doing so, it blends in with the room décor and it is a design that will grow with the child well into his preschool and childhood years.

Before

Maximizing closet space with an organizing system will help you achieve a successful nursery design. The more storage you have for clothes and essential baby items, the less furniture you will need in the room.

Murals are a big trend in nursery décor. They add a personalized touch in the space, but if it's too cost prohibitive to hire a professional artist to achieve this look, decals are one of the best inventions in home décor! There is a wide selection of designs and lettering, which can be applied not only on the walls, but also on furniture, doors and mirrors—almost any surface. The installation is as easy as peel and stick, and the best part is that unlike paint, with decals you have no commitment. Many are removable and repositionable.

Another wall treatment you can consider is wallpaper. It's being used more than ever before, with bold colors, large-scale patterns and to simulate natural finishes such as concrete, marble and more. In the girl's nursery, the beautiful linen wallpaper with striped gray lines remained the focal point behind the crib. The rest of the walls, which were originally white since the bedroom was being used as a guest bedroom, received a new coat of paint in a soft pale pink.

Particularly in this section on walls I also want to address the closet doors. If the width of your closet takes up an entire wall span similar to the girl's nursery, then for all intents and purposes it can be considered a wall. The doors were 8-feet (2.5-m) tall and plain, so paint alone would not create the effect I wanted for this glam-inspired nursery. The solution was to upholster the front of the doors with a quilted, soft pink fabric trimmed with piping and finished with a diamond stud in the center of each of the tufted panels. It made the closet doors one of the design features in this nursery. Yet another idea to transform an existing closet door is to install mirrored inserts in the panels. Mirrors are a great way to make a room appear bigger and also add an elegant style, which will be useful and timeless.

2 Furniture

Okay, so here it goes: Before you even think about buying furniture for the nursery, my advice is to give the closet in the room a makeover! Yes, trust me on this. Why buy additional, unnecessary furniture for the nursery, which might cram up the room, when you can take full advantage of the closet to organize all the baby clothes. The less furniture in the room, the better because eventually you will also need the floor space for all the toys and for the child to play in his or her room. I'm a big fan of having a closet organizing system in every room, but even more so in a nursery for this reason.

There are many DIY options at your local home improvement store. You can invest in a custom system with shelves and drawers, which will eliminate the need to buy other pieces of furniture just for baby clothes and blankets. Maximize the inside of the closet by using all the vertical walls and empty spaces underneath. You can also place inexpensive cube bookcases on the bottom, which is great for toys, shoes, books and so much more.

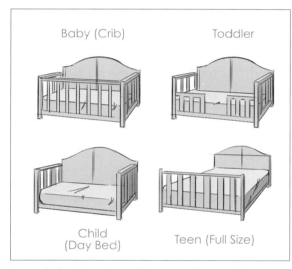

Baby (Crib)   Toddler

Child
(Day Bed)   Teen (Full Size)

Invest in furniture that will grow with your baby through the years such as a convertible crib.

Convertible Furniture

In theory, the three essential furniture pieces you need in a nursery are a crib, changing table and glider. When it comes time to pick out the specific furniture, it's best to buy pieces designed to grow with your child, such as convertible cribs and changing tables that can easily transition to a stand-alone dresser with the simple removal of the topper. The topper is a separate piece that attaches to the top of the dresser to securely hold a contour pad to change a baby. Some have compartments that allow you to organize diapers, creams and other necessities.

Thinking ahead will save you lots of money in the future. For example, the two-toned dresser in gray and white in the girl's nursery has clean lines and a modern style that can really work in any bedroom no matter the age of the child. As for a crib, shop for a model that can convert into a toddler bed, daybed and a full-size bed—all the while keeping the same headboard and footboard by purchasing side rails separately.

Before

Gliders

A must-have for a new mom is a glider or rocker. I like incorporating rockers that don't necessarily look as if they are designed for a baby room. At first glance they resemble a beautiful accent chair you can place anywhere in your home. The many fabric selections and styles now available allow you to do just that.

In the boy's nursery the tufted wingback chair is modern and still takes into account the nursing mother's needs. In the future, the glider can also be converted into a traditional armchair by placing stationary feet on it. Love this look! In comparison, the glider in the girl's nursery resembles a comfy, oversized accent chair. In both vignettes the addition of an upholstered, round ottoman placed at the foot of the glider makes the seating that much more comfortable and also eliminates sharp corners as the baby begins to crawl.

Side tables are a good place to keep items handy while nursing or reading a bedtime story. They don't have to match the nursery furniture and are more practical when they are the same height as the arm of the glider.

Accent Tables

With every sitting corner I create in a nursery, I always place an accent table or side table next to the glider. This becomes a stylish addition in the room that can be a totally different finish or style from the crib and dresser, so that everything doesn't coordinate perfectly. It's also practical because it allows you to place a cute lamp for ambient lighting, baby bottles during feeding or a frame with a photo of your prince or princess. The wood and metal side table in the boy's nursery adds warmth and is a nice contrast to the rest of the furniture in white. In a similar manner, the polished aluminum table screams elegance with a touch of Hollywood glam when combined with the lamp on top featuring a metal shade with crystal pendants.

Side tables become a fun accent in the nursery. Keep the scale of the table small with just enough surface space to set items on near the glider. Stay away from buying a matching nightstand to the furniture set. They tend to be too low and too bulky to place next to a glider. A visual reference is to have the surface of the side table be at the same height as the arm of the glider or taller.

Secure Furniture

Most manufacturers of nursery furniture include an anti-tip kit. It's basically a nylon strap and mounting hardware that secures tall or heavy pieces to the wall, preventing them from toppling over. It's something new parents don't necessarily think about initially when decorating a nursery, but for obvious reasons it's priceless to maintain a safe environment for your baby or toddler and prevent accidents. Take an extra moment to brace all tippable furniture to the wall when putting the nursery together initially rather than waiting until later when the baby begins to crawl.

3 Accessories

Do you find yourself visiting the baby store and wanting to buy all the pieces in a collection? It's okay to be inspired, but less is more. Most parents like coming up with a theme for their baby's room: the two most common being a princess room for girls and sports for boys. I totally get it. There's nothing wrong with this as long as you don't make the mistake of being too literal and go overboard. This is where the accessories can either support your inspiration or turn the nursery into a theme park. It becomes a theme park when you buy all the coordinating accessories in the matching print to the bedding. You know what I'm talking about, right? Baby stores make it so easy for new parents to succumb to this when they stock the shelves with the coordinating lamp shades, valances, curtains, pillows, area rug . . . and it goes on and on. Definitely don't do the matching wallpaper border—I beg of you.

To achieve a designer look, the secret is not to match the same print in everything you buy; instead, mix it up with coordinating colors/solids and add the print in subtle ways to bring it all together, such as a throw pillow or wall art. Keeping the theme to accents in the room will be much easier to switch out when the baby becomes a toddler and outgrows the décor.

Accessories on the wall and throughout the nursery tie in the color scheme and whimsical theme of fairytales and adventure.

The inspiration for the boy's nursery was a tribal-adventure theme. The bedding itself featured whimsical safari animals against a modern backdrop, and a sense of adventure was brought into the room with a teepee tent and other inspirational artwork on the walls. Notice how all the details in the décor reflect a theme of jungle and exploration without having the need to use animals everywhere in the room.

The girl's nursery was an interpretation of a modern princess room without seeing castles and tiaras everywhere in the décor either. The room has elements of glamour and elegance with a sophisticated color palette of pink, gray and white. These are examples of how a nursery design can reflect a theme without being repetitive with all the decorative accessories.

Artwork

Murals and lightweight canvas prints are good options as artwork—especially above the crib for safety reasons. I also like to feature beautiful lifestyle photos captured throughout the pregnancy as a way to personalize the space. Refrain from putting artwork on every single wall; instead, create groupings of frames in different sizes on one wall as a focal point. A cute idea is to use the actual baby clothes as art on the walls. Hang them from a decorative hook or place inside a picture frame without the glass. It's decorative and functional at the same time to plan baby outfits. A fun, oversized clock can also do double duty. You can keep track of naps and feeding times, but it enhances the décor of the nursery. The wood and metal clock I used adds texture and warmth and ties into other metal finishes in the room such as the ceiling fan, side table and knobs. Take full advantage of the wall with shelves, bookcases and baskets that allow you to display toys, books and other favorite accessories in the room as actual décor while clearing clutter off the floors.

Stylish Knobs

Subtle changes can make a difference in the style of furniture. To give a store-bought piece a more custom look, change out the drawer knobs and pulls. It's an inexpensive update. By switching the white, wood knobs on the dresser to bronze, the style went from country to more contemporary. There are assortments of knobs you can buy at any home improvement store, and they also make great decorative hooks on the wall.

Area Rug

An area rug is another layering piece in a nursery. It can pull all the colors together and make a room inviting and cozy. If you have wood or tile floors, I recommend placing an area rug down to warm up the hard surface. Even if you have wall-to-wall carpet, you can still consider a rug, too. The trick is to contrast the textures when placing an area rug over carpet, which I'm totally not against. If your carpet is low pile, you can add a shag or free-form-shape rug on top of it, like a plush sheepskin or hide. The reverse holds true if you have thicker carpet; opt for rugs with a tighter weave. Regardless of your subfloor, area rugs usually become a focal point in the center of the room since most traditional layouts in a nursery have the furniture up against the walls.

The same rules we follow in a living room apply when choosing a size of rug; however, you can also add smaller accent rugs in the room if you wish to define a certain area. In the boy's nursery, I placed a small, faux flokati (sheepskin) rug inside the teepee. The shaggy pile is soft and comfortable for the baby to play on as he grows older. I used a similar pink wool version in the girl's nursery underneath a comfy chair to define the cozy corner. It's a simple touch that adds an understated layer of luxury.

Choosing the design of the rug can either make or break the overall look of the nursery. Think of it as designing an outfit. If you have too many patterns from head to toe, the look might clash. On the flip side, if you wear solids from head to toe, it might read as boring. The trick is to find the right balance so the area rug complements the style of the nursery. I went with a modern geometric rug in the boy's nursery that picked up on the colors in the bedding. I didn't want a busy pattern or print that would compete with the mural and bedding motif. I must admit, though, the honeycomb design reminded me subliminally of a giraffe print, so I went with it. I wasn't being literal; I follow my own rules. In the girl's nursery it was all about blending the floors with the overall serenity and elegance of the room, so I chose a soft pink, diamond trellis design. The pattern was subtle enough to provide visual interest without commanding too much attention.

Lighting

As in all spaces in a home, lighting options in a nursery vary from ambient to task lighting. In the boy's nursery I used a modern three-blade ceiling fan mainly as a decorative element since the room already had lots of recessed lighting and central A/C. It has real cherrywood blades with an LED light, which is energy efficient and also dimmable. The reason I chose this style is because it reminded me of a propeller on a plane, which becomes a subtle reference to the theme of the room: travel and adventure. I also included a cute table lamp next to the glider—the base added a pop of color on the wood side table and the burlap of the lamp shade kept the light source masculine. For ambience, I completed the lighting with a whimsical elephant lamp on the dresser/changing table.

Staying true to an elegant and modern style, the chandelier lamp on the aluminum side table in the girl's nursery was inspired by the ceiling fixture already installed in the room. It was a sheer, pleated drum shade with crystal pendants, so I wanted to tie the looks together. However, I didn't want to create the look of a matching set, which is the reason I chose this particular lamp with a metal shade. Think ahead and make sure to use plug protectors to cover any unused outlets.

Window Treatments

When you have a baby, the ability to control the natural light coming into the nursery is of utmost importance for napping and overall comfort. The window treatments should complement the décor, but also be functional for this very purpose, filtering direct sunlight. You have beautiful options ranging from panels, shades or valances, or you can use a combination of any of these to dress up the windows.

For a simpler look inside the window casing, fabric shades can add pattern and color and are available with linings that block sound and light. I know the more popular alternative is to install blinds, which is fine for controlling the light, but they don't offer much in terms of style. My personal preference is to layer the blinds with fabric panels on either side to frame the window as I did in the boy's nursery. Look for blackout curtains that darken and keep the room cooler. Another option is to install a decorative valance across the top to soften the look along with the blinds.

Regardless of which style you choose, safety is important whenever you have window coverings, so make sure any cords are out of reach or look for styles that are cordless.

Design Your Life

When it comes to designing spaces in a home, I believe a nursery has a deeper level of emotional connection for the parents. Before a single piece of furniture is placed, the room already represents the hopes and dreams of a family growing by another generation. It's where the past intersects with the present as it looks to the future. If you stop for a moment and think about that, it makes you realize how pretty amazing life is.

As adults, sometimes you forget that you were once a baby too and that your parents were living the same moment you are today many years ago. Now their baby is having a baby of their own and the legacy continues. You might have this awareness already, but I think it's worth a reminder as you begin to decorate the nursery, because it's a special moment in time.

The family history can also be expressed in the nursery décor with items that belonged to mommy and daddy: create a gallery display with beautiful black-and-white baby portraits, add shadow boxes with your first pair of shoes or display a vintage toy you had as a child that maybe your parents saved to pass along to their grandchildren. It's accessories like these that are priceless for the memories they carry. It's a nod to the past that fills the nursery with so much love for what the future holds.

Personalized Artwork

There is nothing cuter than personalizing a nursery with the baby's name, right? In this makeover, the wall was empty and needed artwork to create a focal point. With simple materials from an arts and crafts store, we can make a custom frame collection that will be extra special because it was made with so much love.

Monograms, initials and personalized items are a big trend in home décor, and even more so when it comes time to decorate a nursery. The baby's name can be added to pillows, furniture, lamps, toys and so much more. The challenge is to only use them in one or two accents in the room and refrain from overwhelming the space with too much personalization. When used correctly in the design, it's a décor detail that can make the room feel even more special for your bundle of joy.

These one-of-a-kind pieces are usually a custom order and depending on where you source the merchandise, it can also get expensive. I came up with this DIY project when I was decorating a nursery and needed a way to make an impact without spending too much. Instead of framing paper initials inside, I used the matted frame as the backdrop to a wood letter I adhered to the outside. This made the artwork three-dimensional and gave it more presence on the wall.

The personalized artwork can also be updated to coordinate with different color schemes as the baby grows by simply switching out the scrapbooking paper inside the frame, so it will never become obsolete in the room design. The best part is you made it!

Materials

Spray paint

9" (23-cm) wood letters—spelling out the baby's name

Scrapbooking paper—various patterns and colors

11" x 14" (28 x 35.5-cm) photo frames— buy as many as you need to spell out the baby's name

Sheer ribbon

Staple gun

Foam mounting double-sided tape

Decorative knobs

Hanger bolts

Plastic anchors

Cordless drill

Steps

1. Begin by spray painting the letters in a color of your choice, if you'd like. I used a soft gray. It's best to use spray paint for even coverage. Make sure you do this outside in a well-ventilated area.

2. Place a different scrapbooking sheet inside each of the frames. You have the option of keeping the 8 x 10-inch (20.5 x 25.5-cm) mat and placing the scrapbooking sheet behind it, which is what I did, or you can cover the entire 11 x 14-inch (28 x 35.5-cm) frame with the sheet to reveal more of the pattern.

3. Turn the frames over. Cut the ribbon into 20-inch (51-cm) strips and staple each end to the top center of the frame edge with 5-inch (13 cm) spacing in between. Do this on all the frames.

4. Before you adhere the letters on the front, pay close attention to the colors of the scrapbooking sheets inside the frame. It's best to separate similar colors to avoid having them side by side on the wall. Arrange the colors in order of how the name will be spelled out. In the project, I used different tones of pink and fuchsia with a subtle pattern.

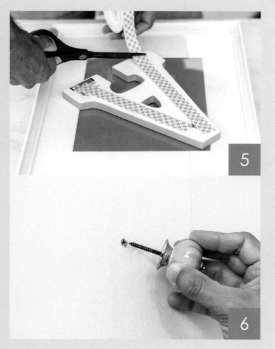

5. Secure the wood letters onto the front and center on the frame using the foam mounting double-sided tape. Distribute the tape evenly to ensure good contact on the glass.

6. For the hook, I used a decorative knob to hang the frames from the ribbon. You might have to replace the screw that came with the knob with a hanger bolt, which has a wood screw on one end that threads into the wall using a plastic anchor, and a machine screw on the other end that threads into the knob. I drilled the hole for the plastic anchor with a cordless drill. Hangar bolts vary in sizes depending on the knob you choose, so be aware of this, but you can find them at your local hardware store.

7. Space the frames evenly on the wall and hang by tying a bow around the knob to complete the whimsical display.

After

The collection of frames now becomes an art installation on the nursery wall. At a certain point when the child is older, the frames can still be used for photos by simply removing the letters, so it's a smart design and money well spent.

Before

CHAPTER 6

Teen Bedrooms
Making It Fun & Creative While Keeping It Neat & Tidy

I remember when I got the chance to decorate my own bedroom as a teenager. It was a blank slate to express myself. I felt proud of every color choice, furniture and artwork I placed on the walls, which included many Madonna posters. In hindsight, it was my first step into the design world that, unbeknownst to me at the time, I'd turn into a career many years later. I feel passionate about involving kids in the decorating process of their personal space because it's part of the home environment that shapes the person they become. They might not realize it consciously, but how they express themselves through décor, I believe, can impact their scholastic and adolescent formative years. It's more obvious when kids start choosing what they wear because you begin to see their personal style emerging through their wardrobe; you get the essence of the person by seeing how they dress, and in a similar occurrence it happens with their bedroom décor.

Generally speaking, the parents as the adults, and in many cases before children are even born, choose the decorating style of the home—both exterior and interior. It's indirectly imposed on the children growing up and understandably so. However, as your child gets older and starts to voice that they want input in how their bedroom should look, it's important that Mom and Dad listen and guide them in their décor choices. It's a form of self-expression as they develop their own sense of personal identity.

1 Walls

Does the décor in your child's bedroom still reflect your choices from years ago when they were a little boy or girl? Now, as adolescents, do you feel the space represents who they are becoming as young adults and their current interests? It could be that their school colors, favorite sports teams or hobbies can be the new inspiration to update the design of their bedroom.

When I walked into this teenager's bedroom, I could already get a sense of who she was based on some of the elements I found in the room. She hung a large Mandala tapestry print on the wall and had taken "artistic liberty" by drawing on the furniture. I knew immediately which direction she wanted to go, and who she was—artsy, creative and eclectic—but it wasn't being expressed fully in her bedroom décor, yet. I envisioned a boho-chic style, which is very popular among girls. It reflects a bohemian, free-spirited design that layers textures, prints and colors; it mixes old and new elements for a casual, world-traveled look.

The first step to tackle on the walls was paint. The existing ivory wasn't fun or youthful. Being that the main focal point of the bedroom was the tapestry, we used that as our inspiration piece for the color scheme and painted all the walls a robin's egg blue, influenced by the iconic color of the famous Tiffany jewelry brand. By way of paint alone, a style factor began to emerge in the environment. Soft hues of blues, greens and aquas are colors that remind us of the sea and sky, evoking a tranquil vibe in a bedroom. It was the perfect color choice to create a modern boho-chic bedroom.

Daybeds, bunk beds and loft-style beds can maximize the square footage of a teen bedroom. It frees up valuable floor space, which can make the room appear bigger.

2 Furniture

It's safe to say that at this stage, the nursery furniture that transitioned them well into their toddler and pre-adolescent years is no longer appropriate for young adults. Similar to their wardrobe style, which now is more trendy and fashionable, their furniture can also reflect a cool and modern vibe. As you begin to shop for new furnishings, pay close attention to how they use the overall space and how their bedroom can support their lifestyle and activities.

In most cases, teen rooms need to function as a studio apartment of sorts. They have to be a multifunctional space that supports different needs—from sleeping to studying and everything in between, as it becomes a hangout space for friends, too. With this in mind, furniture plays an important role to do all these activities. In the makeover, I only kept the platform bed and the chest of drawers that at first glance seemed unusable. It was solid wood and I knew it could be rescued with paint to give it a custom look.

Bed

Choosing the style and size of the bed depends on the square footage of the room. The two most popular sizes in teen spaces are twin and full. Both decisions should also take into account if the room is going to be shared by siblings since you don't want the room to look like mattress city. There are clever designs that allow you to create sleeping quarters for more than one person without taking up valuable floor space.

Daybeds are a great option for smaller spaces. They open up the floor plan and mimic the look of a sofa when placed up against the wall. You can also include a trundle underneath with an additional mattress for sleepovers or use the space as storage for toys, sheets, shoes and clothes. You can find daybeds in many materials for both girls and boys that include wrought-iron, upholstered and wood frames.

Before

Bunk beds are also space efficient and a favorite among children for their bedroom—especially if the room is shared by two. The height of the ceiling needs to be considered, and it is recommended that you have about 2 feet (61 cm) between the top of the bunk bed and ceiling. In the same category are loft beds. These offer a lot of features depending on how the bedroom will be used. For example, you can combine a bed on top with a study area below or use both areas for sleeping. They can be a cool experience for your child, which is why it's important to involve them in the decision.

Regardless of which bed style you choose, explore additional features like pull-out drawers or mattresses that lift up with hydraulics, revealing valuable storage compartments.

Nightstands

Mixing nightstand styles is a form of expressing personality. I chose two side tables in the same color, but different shapes for an eclectic look where nothing is a perfect match. The nightstands are practical and stylish by having one storage drawer, and the details of the routed edges and turned legs give a nod to a French influence. The pieces feel more collected this way. The scale of the tables is smaller and adds to the charm because it's not your typical bedroom nightstand that is much wider. This is also the reason I placed one on either side of the bed; but if the room is used by one child you really don't need two nightstands at all. Save the money. You can still create symmetry on the bed wall by placing a bookcase or desk or reading chair on the opposite side, making better use of the space—especially if the square footage is limited.

Certainly the nightstand can match the bedroom set, but my suggestion is to only buy one. Think outside the box and add a pop of color and texture with an accent table or woven tray table to create a unique look.

Chest

The chest of drawers received its own makeover of sorts by painting the drawer fronts in different colors and switching out the knobs. This is where took inspiration from the original attempt by the teenager to draw on the furniture and decided to enhance her vision, which makes it a feature in the bedroom. I also used different knob styles on each drawer to reflect that cool, bohemian look. It's a conversation piece that cannot be store-bought. Buying unfinished wood furniture is not only less expensive, but it's a nice way for your child to place their own artistic stamp on the project by personalizing the piece as they see fit.

Stylish Desk

Alas, we all know a teen's bedroom is not just for sleeping or socializing with friends; it must also be used for studying and doing homework. Incorporating a study area is a requirement to make this space functional and productive. I gave a store-bought desk more presence by adding a glass top. Most furniture stores sell glass tops alone, so it's a great way to take a simple desk and make it more special—plus the glass does double duty: it protects the surface from scratches and you can use the area in between the desk and glass to display photos and other collectibles. Combining two console tables along one wall is another way to create a stylish work zone.

Desk as a Vanity

When floor space is limited, the desk can also be used in different ways. In a girl's bedroom it becomes a practical vanity by placing a marquee makeup mirror on it or hanging a beautiful framed mirror on the wall above it. It maximizes the floor space by having one piece of furniture do double duty. Plus, I also think it looks cool and modern. Nowadays most kids/teenagers have a laptop so there is no need for extra computer equipment that will take up room on the surface. If you are using it as a vanity or to do craft projects, it helps to have a glass top to make the cleanup easier.

Before

Desk as a Nightstand

I touched upon this idea in the nightstand section, but yet another way you can use a desk is as a nightstand. Desk width sizes vary, so you can find the right fit to place next to a bed and balance out the traditional nightstand on the other side. Mind you, keeping it organized is essential because it becomes part of the bedroom's focal point with the bed, so use pencil caddies, magazine holders and storage boxes to maintain the area neat and tidy. You'll be more productive when you have everything handy and there is no clutter on the desk.

Chair

The desk chair can also make an impression in the bedroom. Specifically, if you're using the desk as a vanity, the chair needs to have an equally Hollywood-glam aesthetic. In most of the girls' bedroom makeovers I tend to use a comfy and armless upholstered dining chair. You can coordinate the fabric to the color scheme of the room, and by the chair being armless it allows you to easily pull the chair underneath the desk while you're working. I'm not against using an industrial office chair—especially if you need features like fully adjustable height and caster wheels—but this style mainly works in a modern setting. I recommend that you look for a sleek design with a low back, so it doesn't compete with the desk and complements the style of the bedroom.

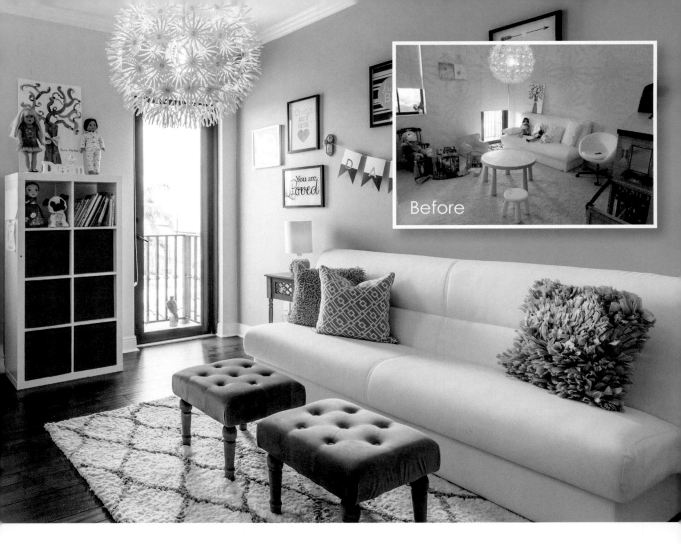
Before

Hanging Out in Style

When you create a space that you love, of course you're going to want to invite your friends over to hang out. Boys' and girls' bedrooms need to function as a cool space to lounge, too, and there are few ways to achieve this other than sitting on the bed.

In one of the makeovers, I combined two separate pieces to create the look of a built-in bench (see right-most photo on page 152). I purchased an upholstered headboard I found in the clearance section at a furniture store and hung it directly on the wall, leaving enough room underneath for a bench. With the throw pillows and side table I created a fashionable and functional sitting area for less.

Other options include a comfy loveseat or accent chair with ottoman in a corner of the room and oversized floor pillows and beanbags on the area rug.

Shelving Units

There can never be enough storage, and that's especially true in a child's bedroom. Modular shelving units are inexpensive and allow you to create a custom look depending on your needs. You can add doors, drawers or baskets to any of the cubby holes for instant hidden storage. You can find these shelving units in many colors and sizes and you can use them horizontally or vertically. When you place them on the floor, the top surface can be used as a media console or dresser; and when it's vertical against the wall, it's a good way to take advantage of the height of the room for books, accessories or sports equipment. Modular pieces are ideal when you need the space to be multifunctional.

3 Accessories

The accessories in a kid's bedroom do more than just finish the look of the space. They are also a direct reflection of the real passions and interests of the child—more so than paint or furniture. This is how you get a true sense of who they are and what they like at that particular moment in their lives. Their possessions are connected to their identity, and displaying them is a way of celebrating that. The trophies, photographs, drawings, books and more take on a whole new meaning when we see it from this perspective.

Fundamentally, this also applies to how adults decorate every room and why we surround ourselves with our belongings. It's one of those realizations that make you stop for a moment to ponder the deeper connection we have to objects in our home.

Bedding

Bedding is everything in a teen bedroom since it makes a style statement. It's a great way to add personality in the room. Depending on the age of the child, you want to consider how easy it is to clean because there's a big possibility the bed will eventually be used as a trampoline or spills might happen from eating snacks. Duvet covers and coverlets are a good option because the lightweight materials can be cleaned in a standard washing machine. Heavier comforters might require front-loading machines or even dry cleaning.

Dressing the bed can become as fun as picking out an outfit. Bedding sets that bring all the coordinating accessories make it easy, but make sure to add other patterns and solids to break up the uniformity. You know I'm not a big fan of the "matchy-matchy" look.

In the boho-chic inspiration room I used a mandala print on the duvet with coordinating shams, then added more pattern and texture with an array of throw pillows. At first glance you might think so many patterns might be too busy, but it all works to create a cool, gypsy-like space.

Throw Pillows

Throw pillows can be just as expressive as the bedding itself. With so many fun colors and styles, they almost become a must-have novelty in a teen bedroom. It's a youthful version of a grown-up bed. The mix of patterns and shapes give the room more personality—everything from emoji faces to their favorite sweets can be quirky. I love combining faux fur pillows with beaded details for a glam look; or shaggy textures with round neck rolls and even fringes for an eclectic feel. The color scheme can tie back to the bedding and allows for customization, such as painting initials or iron-on transfers on inexpensive pillow covers. If there's a favorite team jersey, stitch the seams and stuff it with fiber fill for a one-of-kind decorator pillow.

At night the pillows might end up on the floor, but it's okay. In the morning, it'll be an incentive for the teen to make the bed and properly display them again in their décor—at least we hope!

Artwork

The main artwork in the inspiration room was the Mandala tapestry. However, instead of draping it on the wall like before, I stretched the fabric over a wood frame I created to give it a more refined appearance. This is easy to do by pulling the fabric taut on all sides and stapling it onto the back of the frame. In essence this also became my headboard since the mattress was only sitting on a platform.

Typography and cool accessories that keep you organized become artwork and personalize the walls in a teen bedroom.

I also love the typography trend in home décor that incorporates inspirational phrases in the artwork. The positive messages are pick-me-ups for the soul. It's like free therapy. You can create an entire gallery wall with different quotes, spell out your child's name or add initials to make a stronger statement that is personal to your child.

Cork and magnetic boards keep the space near a desk organized, but they also become art for the walls when you buy them beautifully framed. I'm also including shelves and shadow boxes in this category because you can configure them in many ways to create a grouping that is visually pleasing on the wall and thus, can be considered art. This becomes a display area for the many trophies, art projects and photo frames; sports equipment or wardrobe essentials (e.g., purses or heels) can be exhibited in such a manner that they, too, become part of the artwork in the room.

Mirrors are an inexpensive way to decorate and reflect the natural light in a room. A floor-length mirror can fill an area nicely on a wall and add a bit of drama and glam in the space. Smaller versions can be hung above a desk to create a vanity or above a bookcase to create a dresser. You can also hang ornamental mirrors in interesting shapes like sunburst, quatrefoil, frameless and more, which add to the style of the room as a decorative element.

Area Rug

Area rugs add another layer of color and texture in the design. In a kid's bedroom you don't have to necessarily abide by all the size guidelines I shared in the Bedroom Suite chapter (page 86) because you're designing a more carefree space. The main thing to keep in mind is the style of the area rug.

In the boho-chic makeover I featured a solid gray faux flokati rug at the foot of the bed, so that it wouldn't compete with all the patterns in the room. Flokati rugs, very popular in the '60s and '70s, are handmade shag wool rugs that add a soft texture to a room. It's often been said that everything old eventually comes back into style, and this adage definitely holds true with design trends. The retro rug filled the otherwise empty space on the floor between the bed and desk area.

This is quite a contrast to another makeover where I used an 8 x 10-foot (2.5 x 3-m) area rug to almost cover the entire flooring. Even though the bedding had a pattern, the gray background made it neutral, whereby I could still use a bold color with the damask print on the area rug. The two prints were also different sizes, and this is the secret to mixing patterns in the same area.

You can also get more creative with the placement of the area rug in the room and choose a diagonal layout slightly underneath the bed. This works for smaller spaces when you wish to break up the straight lines of the room.

Lighting

Traditional light sources include overhead fixtures, lamps on nightstands and task lighting on a desk. The best part is they can all make their own individual statement in the bedroom, beginning with the fixture on the ceiling as a beautiful focal point.

The fixture in the boho-chic makeover has an artistic quality with the look of blown glass. It features teardrops and garland strands that project decorative patterns on the wall and ceilings when the light bounces off the crystals. The style is elegant, like something you would see in a Parisian villa, which captures the eclectic design of the room. This chandelier was already in the room before the makeover, so it was a second source of design inspiration. I complemented the overhead light with a modern table lamp on the nightstands. The brushed nickel, stacked spheres on the base and embroidered drum shades add visual interest and diffuse the light.

Whether it's task or mood lighting, the point is having fun choosing a lamp depending on the room's décor. There is a wide selection of styles including up lights, globes, lava lamps and LEDs; even strings of light can add ambience and a nice glow in a child's bedroom.

Organization

I know keeping things organized can be a challenge in a kid's room, but the right decorative elements might just motivate them to do so. Desk accessories, jewelry organizers and decorative trays are available in fun patterns and fabrics that enhance the décor of the room. A tray placed on a dresser is great for lotions and perfumes; you can even use it on a nightstand to change up the look. Bins and baskets with lids in vibrant colors can be incorporated on a bookcase, nightstand or chest, providing additional hidden storage.

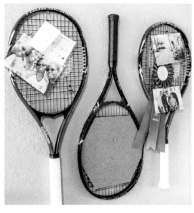

This all goes back to incorporating double-duty furniture similar to cubby bins that you can adapt with baskets and doors based on your storage needs. College dorm trunks make great side tables and can also be used as benches for additional seating. Most importantly, you can pack a lot of stuff inside, such as blankets, seasonal clothes and sports equipment. Try to utilize any extra space in the room with underbed storage containers for shoes and clothing; if necessary, add hanging fabric shelves in the closet for sweaters, jeans and more. These pieces can be bought in fun colors, so they can coordinate with the décor, too—aside from being space-saving items.

Get creative and use accessories like hats and sports equipment as actual décor by hanging them from hooks or displaying on shelves. A collection on a wall or on the front of closet doors can turn these basic items into a cool, artistic installation. This ensures that all your essentials remain accessible, while keeping the bedroom organized and stress-free.

In a boho-chic design, a mix of patterns, textures and colors reflect an eclectic style where nothing is a matching set, yet it all works together in the room.

Window Treatments

In the boho-chic room, I had to be careful not to add another print that might clash with the wall tapestry and bedding. There was enough going on between those two elements. Although this particular design inspiration allows you to mix lots of patterns together, there has to be a subtle restraint to not go overboard. The choice was a gray trellis design against a white backdrop. It dressed up the window and made an elegant statement against the robin's egg blue on the walls. It also unified the color palette of the bedroom by tying in the grays found in the desk chair, lamp shades and area rug.

Striped window panels are another good option if you have bedding with a busy pattern. It will add the right amount of design detail without having to settle with a plain solid. The pink and white panels were the perfect addition in the teen bedroom to balance out all the pink accents throughout the room including the nightstand, area rug and other accessories. The wide stripes are modern and sophisticated behind the bed—without it looking juvenile, which can be the fear for many using pink. Vertical stripes make a room appear taller, while horizontal stripes can make the window seem wider.

Design Your Life

As a kid, I would do my homework on the kitchen peninsula. I never really had a dedicated area in my bedroom for studying until I was in high school. The extent of having my own desk was when I would play "make-believe" office with my brother on the bed with basic supplies like a stapler and folders that I would borrow from my dad. My brother used to pretend he was a teacher, and I supported his imagination since we shared a bedroom. I loved it, though. It made us feel grown up as if we had a professional job.

I believe, through décor, parents can support their kid's creativity early on by creating a work space in their bedroom where they can be productive in different ways—an area where they are not only learning how to succeed scholastically, but also personally, by nurturing any hobbies or passions they seem to be expressing interest in at a young age. It can be painting, coloring, scrapbooking, sculpting, building blocks and so on.

This is not so difficult to do by dedicating a space in their bedroom as a creative corner. It can have a desk with an ottoman as a chair, a bookcase with colorful storage boxes for organization and the walls can have shelving or corkboard tiles to display their personal artwork proudly. This is not about creating an area for playing, but honing in on a talent that makes them special. When kids/teens feel that their dreams are supported at home, the confidence they gain will help them succeed in life, too.

Before

DIY Design
Painted Furniture

This chest of drawers was a great price at only $35. It had clean lines that can work in any bedroom style and can be used in multiple ways. If you have a piece of furniture that belonged to your child and maybe it's too sentimental to part with, we can give it a modern facelift with this paint project.

Painted furniture is a great way to personalize any space. You can take an old piece and give it a new look; or buy a new piece and give it a custom finish. It's a good project to involve the kids because they are tapping into their creative side and using the furniture as a blank canvas to express themselves.

This project can be done on existing furniture that is stained, but it will require extra steps to prep the piece, like sanding to get all of the glossy finish off and applying primer so the new paint will adhere to the surface. It's much easier to paint when you buy the furniture unfinished in real wood. They are reasonably priced and available in many styles. The cost is even less when assembly is required. It can make a fun statement on its own in a bedroom or dorm, or you can paint many pieces to create a collection. The possibilities are limitless!

Materials

Chest of drawers—choice of furniture

Chalk paint—light blue, teal and turquoise or colors of your choice

Paint trays and foam rollers

Stencil—choice of pattern

Painter's tape

Stencil brushes

Brushed metallic paint—gold

Decorative knobs

Steps

1. The piece doesn't have to be primed or sanded since it's unfinished, but before you apply paint, wipe off any dust or particles with a damp cloth.

2. Take the drawers out and paint each front a different shade of blue to create a monochromatic color scheme. This also reflects an ombré effect by layering the colors from light to dark. You can use any color combination you like best that complements your space. Apply the paint with foam rollers for a smoother finish; they are also disposable when you're done.

3. Once the paint is dry, align all the drawers and start with the stencil design in the center and work your way down the entire surface. This will ensure the pattern is repeated evenly for a contiguous look. Hold the stencil in place with painter's tape to prevent it from moving. Dip the tip of the stencil brush in the gold paint and then dab off excess on a scrap piece of paper or cardboard. Apply the paint using the stippling method, which involves dapping the brush against stencil openings. Stencils work best when you build the color to avoid having the paint bleed underneath.

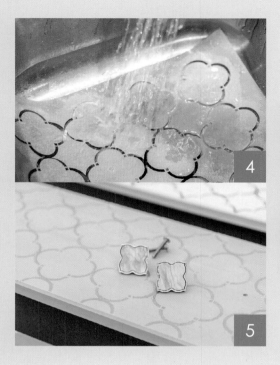

4. As you move from one area to another, it's also suggested that you wash the stencil with soap and water to maintain the crisp lines of the pattern since paint can accumulate from continuous use. Continue overlapping the stencil to complete the design on the sides.

5. I painted the top and sides in a solid color to complete the look. Instead of using the wood knobs the piece originally came with, I added brass knobs with a marble inlay for a touch of modern glam.

After

For less than $100 in materials, you have a custom piece of furniture that can be used as a nightstand next to a bed, media cabinet for a small television, chest for clothes and so much more. It's stylish, budget friendly and a project your kid/teen would enjoy making to decorate their bedroom.

Before

CHAPTER 7

Home Offices
Be Your Own Boss and Work in a Space That Inspires You

One of the many challenges in life is balancing work and home. This can be made even more difficult when you bring work home, or in many cases, actually work from home, because the boundaries become blurred. It can lead to your home becoming a constant reminder of the many things you have to do and mental clutter.

In the past, a home office was associated as a space needed only by an executive or business professional to be able to work from home. It conjured up images of dark, wood-paneled walls; a bulky, ornate desk; a high-back, leather office chair; and of course, a brass banker's desk lamp with a green glass shade to complete the look.

Nowadays, a home office can have a personality of its own. It can be a stylish and creative space where we can be productive and keep our lives organized—a place where we can work, study or simply use the computer. Having a dedicated space for a home office has become as necessary as a kitchen or bathroom for modern living.

If you have a room for this very purpose, the biggest mistake to avoid is that homeowners don't decorate this space to complement the rest of their home's décor. Instead, what I find is furniture that is very "office-looking" as if it belongs in a cubicle at their office building and lots of disorganization that can subconsciously be counter-productive. Why would I want my surroundings at home to remind me of the same setting as my 9 to 5 work life? This is your opportunity to be the boss, to be your own creative director of sorts, and create an inspiring space that strikes the perfect balance between function and style.

The two most important elements when designing a home office are space planning and organization. This office space certainly needed help in both departments. The room was cramped with furniture, all the papers and office supplies were completely exposed, and it seemed more like a storage room than a home office. The nicest thing was the desk, but you couldn't really appreciate it because of all the clutter around it.

1 Walls

Is your home office cluttered with too much furniture? It could be you're not maximizing the vertical space of the room, which will make your space more efficient. What I mean by this is the walls can be treated as both a decorative and functional element in the design. They are decorative because with paint and artwork you can express your personality and have the home office be an extension of you—more so than you can ever do in a work office at an off-site location. By the same token, properly defining the floor plan for different tasks and taking advantage of the height of the room can actually help you work in a more organized environment.

I began the makeover by first tackling the paint color. The sand-colored walls were okay, but the homeowner was open to a new color scheme, so we decided to paint the room in a beautiful taupe/gray. This was the perfect hue to complement the wood tones in the existing desk and flooring to make the space feel fresh and more contemporary. Before, everything was a brown color scheme, so the room fell flat with no contrast.

There's a misconception that if a room is small you should stay away from dark colors. There are other variables that you also have to take into consideration in addition to the square footage of the room. First, how much natural light does the room get and second, how tall is your ceiling. If you have 10-foot (3-m) or higher ceilings you can get away with a darker color, which can make the room cozier.

This being an office for "him," the gray paint color along with the wood and metal accents set the tone for the room. By contrast, the office featured for "her," with pink walls as the backdrop, combines a color scheme of white, black and gold for a more glamorous style. Both are equally productive spaces that reflect the homeowners' personalities, and the paint color set the tone of the home offices.

Assign Each Wall a Task

An important part of space planning is how you wish to use the square footage in a room. In this office space, all the furniture appeared cramped on top of each other mainly due to the scale, but also in large part because the areas were not defined by purpose.

My design plan for the furniture layout in this home office was to assign each wall a specific task. For example, one wall is for the open shelving; another wall is for the TV/media area; yet, another is for the desk. The desk remained floating in the center of the room, but by defining the walls around it and buying furniture in the appropriate scale every wall has its own moment within the space and nothing appears to be converging on top of each other. I even added additional seating with two accent chairs in front of the desk and the room still feels spacious—unlike before I started the makeover.

Before

2 Furniture

When it comes time to furnish a home office, many homeowners think function before style. The main priority becomes finding a suitable desk, file cabinets and bookcases, which are items usually found in this type of setting. Homeowners don't realize initially that the furnishings can be a combination of stylish pieces that coordinate or can be different in a similar manner to how you furnish any other room in your home. I believe the main focus should be to create an environment that is beautiful first; second, it should be a productive space where you can work from home. The secret to achieving this happy medium between form and function is to incorporate furniture that reflects your personal style and keeps your space organized.

The inspiration for the entire design was based on the desk: clean lines with a trestle base, which reflected a transitional style. The wood finish was slightly distressed, which told me the overall look of the room didn't have to be so formal and traditional. This being my design direction, the white dresser and low bookcases were the wrong color and scale for this home office. It completely clashed with the style of the desk, which was the only piece I was keeping in the room. Turns out it was actually furniture from their daughters' playroom when they were kids, so it definitely looked out of place in a masculine office. Aside from the white-washed finish, the furniture didn't take advantage of the height of the room. Yet, another issue was the fact that it provided no hidden storage.

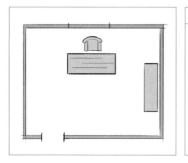 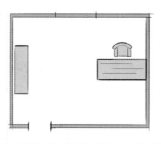 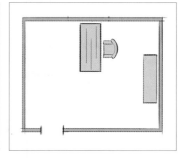

The placement of the desk can impact how you feel about working in your home office. Ideally, place the desk where you have the widest view possible of the room and the door. According to feng shui experts, who practice the Chinese art of the flow of energy, this allows you to take control of your work life since you have greater visibility of the entire room instead of facing a wall.

Desks

Desks can be as unique as the homeowner and are usually the focal point of a home office. There are different styles—ranging from traditional desktop, compact and laptop designs—and choosing the right one will depend on how much space you have in your home office. Ideally, the work surface should be between 20 and 30 inches (51 to 76 cm) deep and the height should be that of a conventional table, about 28 to 30 inches (71 to 76 cm) to sit comfortably. But the width can vary between 24 and 60 inches (61 and 152.5 cm) depending on how you'll use the desk and how much computer equipment will be on the surface. This is where drawing the outline on the floor with painter's tape will help, so you pick a desk that is the right scale to your space.

With any size, make sure there is enough room for your computer monitor, a small table lamp and other accessories that are pretty to look at on the desk, such as photo frames and organizers. Additional features like keyboard storage drawers are nice because they slide out from under the desk, which can save work space on top of your actual table. For smaller rooms, stay away from corner desks that tend to overpower the space because they wrap around two walls. Instead, look for a glass-topped option that reflects light to make the room feel more open and spacious.

The position of the desk will depend on the traffic flow into the room. In the inspiration room, it floats in the center since this space was used by an executive, but if you wish to free up more floor space, position the desk against a wall. Close to a window is ideal because of the natural light, but if this doesn't work with your room's layout, it's best to position your chair to face the door, so your viewpoint is more open and not confined to a solid wall.

Shelving

The first furniture pieces I brought into the room were two tall étagères. This is the fancy name in French for a piece of furniture with open shelving used to display your collectibles and knickknacks. You can call it a bookcase if you want, but the main difference between the two is there is no backing, which is the reason why it's referred to as "open" shelving. I fell in love with these from the moment I saw them at the furniture store, and the best part was they were on clearance and 50 percent off for being a floor model. The original price was $1,000 for each, and I paid that amount for both. If you wish to save money buying new furniture, look for floor models and clearance sections—all furniture stores have them.

By going tall with the étagères, it created a beautiful focal point on the main wall when you first walked into the office. It also took advantage of the ceiling height in the room by drawing your eye up, which made the room feel bigger. The glass shelving within the wood frame kept the étagères from feeling too heavy in the room, too. Aside from being able to display décor and collectibles, it incorporated storage on the two bottom drawers. The depth of the étagères is 18 inches (45.5 cm), which meant it didn't protrude into the center of the room. The ash-brown finish complemented the warm tone of the existing desk without it being a perfect match. It feels more collected in this manner as opposed to looking like a furniture set. It is perfectly fine to mix wood tones provided you keep your choices to two or three types of finishes. Be conscious of this as you shop for furniture and accessories.

Dual-Purpose Tables

On the opposite side of the home office I incorporated a beautiful live edge console table. Live edge refers to the natural edge of the slab of wood used as the tabletop, which becomes a key design feature of the piece. It's rustic and modern all in one, with the exposed grain and natural knots and grain juxtaposed against the stainless steel base. Another key feature of this piece is that it floats off the ground. This is also a designer trick, which can make a room appear more spacious. This console is truly a conversation piece in the room. I love, love, love it underneath the TV to balance out the wall. In another office setting it can also be used as a credenza behind the desk. It's versatile because if you ever want to switch up the décor, you can use it in a living room as a sofa table or media base, in a dining room as a sideboard, or foyer as an entrance table.

In the glam makeover, I used a second long table next to the main desk to give the homeowner an additional work surface. This creates the look of a built-in by keeping all the pieces in the same color against the wall including the filing cabinet. This home office was also used as a guest bedroom with a futon, so it was important to define the room by tasks and keep the two areas—working and sleeping—separate.

Floating Bookcase

Floating shelves are a great alternative to a traditional bookcase. This works nicely if you have limited floor space for furniture because you don't have any legs that rest on the ground; this look also reflects a minimalistic and modern style in the home office.

The word "float" refers to the shelf showing no visible support or bracket because it's hidden within the design. They are available in a variety of widths and finishes and give you the look and function of a vertical bookcase when you install two or three forming a column on the wall. You can also create your own unique design by combining different shelf lengths. You might be surprised to know that I purchase many of these decorative shelves at a home improvement store.

Before

Writing Desk

What happens if I don't have a complete room to be used as a home office and need to borrow space in a bedroom? To be honest, I'm not a big fan of bringing work into a bedroom. As a designer, I believe the two spaces should be kept separate; your bedroom should only be a place of serenity and relaxation. Somehow being reminded about work by having an office desk in the room doesn't quite fit in with that Zen feeling you wish to surround yourself with. Yet, I also understand that due to space limitations in your home this might not be a realistic option.

Therefore, creating a space to work from home doesn't necessarily require that you have a separate room. Be inspired by how hotel rooms incorporate different task areas within the same room, making it a multifunctional space for the guest. You can do the same. This means that if you absolutely need a desk in any bedroom, then the focus needs to shift to creating a beautiful writing desk similar to those you see in a hotel suite. By doing so, you have a functional piece of furniture that also fits in with the bedroom décor.

Find a unique piece that can function as a desk by shopping at antique stores, garage sales and even flea markets. With a little TLC (tender loving care), it can become a special item in the room. Don't be afraid to give any piece you find a facelift by painting it a bold color and making it a modern statement in the room that reflects your personality! The goal is to make the piece stand on its own without resembling a traditional "office" desk. For example, a console table can also function as a desk. It's a perfect size to use with a laptop and a space-saving solution for small rooms.

Keep in mind the chair you choose is just as important. You can use an elegant upholstered dining room chair to function as a desk chair. Incorporate task lighting through a table lamp and add decorative boxes on the surface to store office supplies such as envelopes, stamps, and more. It's important to focus on the "home" aspect in the room when incorporating a writing desk in a bedroom. This means that you don't have to limit yourself to shopping at a big-box office supply store for furnishings.

Neat & Tidy

Keeping things neat and tidy is a big challenge for many in a home office. The first thing I recommend is to convert the closet into storage central. Closet organizing systems are available in different wood finishes and can be used for organizing more than just clothes. Take advantage of the shelving and drawers for papers, office supplies, files, books and so on. Another idea is to remove the closet doors altogether and insert standard bookcases within the dimensions of the opening to create the look of a built-in wall unit. You can personalize the back of the bookcase with paint or wallpaper for a designer look for less.

Avoid the visual clutter that can sometimes happen on the open shelves by using baskets or bins with lids to store smaller items. Each bin or decorative box can be labeled, so you know exactly what is in there at a glance.

3 Accessories

The first thought when it comes to accessorizing a home office might be filling the walls with diplomas, certificates and trophies. Am I right? This can certainly be a part of it as a reminder of your professional accomplishments, but you can also incorporate personal mementos of your life that have just as much meaning. After all, life is a balancing act between the two. In a home office, the decorative accessories don't consist of the stapler and pencil cup holder on the desk either—although I must admit

there are many style options available nowadays that look great. I'm referring to the idea of filling the space with beautiful artwork and décor that feeds your soul and creativity.

In our main inspiration makeover, the homeowner was an avid traveler and his hobby was to fly planes. I incorporated reminders of his passions with references to a world map, airplane models and, of course, family photos throughout the home office. This is where the étagères were transformed with thoughtful groupings and mementos of the homeowner's life and family. The goal was to not clutter the glass shelves but simply to add the right amount of decorative accessories and photos that meant something to the homeowner, so that everything in the room didn't revolve around work.

Artwork in a home office doesn't have to be limited to diplomas, plaques and certificates that only reflect your work life. Have fun mixing in other elements that express your personality!

Boxes and Books

Decorative boxes on the shelves do double duty because they provide a place to store things inside and also act as a pedestal to elevate smaller items to make them more prominent. In this case, it was his daughters' baby shoes preserved in bronze. Using boxes and books in this manner makes the entire collection more important.

Wall Art

The same concept applies to the fabric bulletin boards in the glam-inspired office makeover. It is a decorative element that works as wall art and also provides organization. The bulletin boards are part of a gallery wall grouping that reflects the homeowner's love for fashion and style. They allow you to pin ideas, images or anything else that you like that relates to your work and/or passions.

The focus when it comes to accessorizing the room is to surround yourself with things that make you happy. I even personalized the artwork by displaying her jewelry inside shadow boxes. By doing so, we take something personal and make it that much more special by framing it in such a manner.

Both office makeovers incorporate display ledges to lean photos and artwork. It's a simple way to feature multiple frames without necessarily having to hang them all on the wall. I mix frames in different sizes on the ledges, which adds a lot more visual interest.

Artwork featuring typography and inspirational phrases is another popular design trend we see everywhere, including throw pillows and frames, so I love how the décor can literally inspire and motivate you to be more productive every time you step foot inside your home office. Decals are also a great way to make a bold and graphic statement in a room without the commitment. They are easy to apply and are removable, too. The metallic gold lips decal makes this home office super kissable—at least I think so—which is a reference once again, to the homeowner's love for beauty and glam. Dramatic and modern, with a pop of color all in one.

Lighting

Lighting in a home office can also complement the design. To reflect an industrial style, I went with a fandelier. This is a new phrase coined in the design world referring to a light fixture that combines the beauty of a chandelier with the use of ceiling fan—hence, fandelier. The brushed nickel, drum design fills the gap between the desk and the ceiling. Whoever says ceiling fans are not that exciting (and trust me, I was one of them) has not discovered fandeliers yet and the many styles available. This really was the perfect compromise for this home office.

For additional accent lighting, I placed a replica of an antique pharmacy lamp on the desk. The adjustable arm and lamp head allow you to place light just where you need it for reading or other tasks. The base is compact, making it great for computer stations, and it's visually unobtrusive.

Cord Concealer

Hiding the electrical cords for both the computer and lamp can be tricky when a desk faces out into the room and floats in the center. The solution was to carefully run it down the leg of the desk and then cover the length that goes out into the wall outlet with a neoprene, cord concealer and protector for floors. Not only is it a decorative solution, but it also prevents tripping hazards by leaving the cables exposed. You can buy them in many colors to match your flooring. For the most part, if the location of your desk is next to or in front of a wall you won't have this issue. You can also find desks with a hidden compartment that has a built-in surge protector, so it makes cord management easier and less visible. This is where product design meets function at its best.

Design Your Life

There's a saying that one should work to live and not the other way around. But how many of us are fully conscious of this with the hustle and bustle of everyday life? I know it can be challenging, but it's nice to stop and take a moment to realize this. Yes, we have the weekends as our days off, but even those days fly by and we're back to the manic Mondays beginning another work week to pay the bills.

This is why it's so important to design a home office around your life, your hobbies and your passions, and not necessarily around your work. It should be a beautiful space that surrounds you with inspiration to continue pushing forward and setting goals that you can reach. I'm a firm believer that when you visualize something and put it out in the universe, you will attract it. If you see it, you will achieve it. There's a second saying that I also hold true, which is when you love what you do, it doesn't feel like work. The reality, though, is most people work jobs that are not aligned with their passion. Therefore, I believe that when you walk into a home office that you love, the work doesn't seem as daunting because you've created an environment that supports your spirit and vision first. How you choose to work from home is the one thing you can control.

It's typical to fill your home office with family photos, awards and accomplishments so they serve as a reminder of why you work so hard to begin with. Also, fill it with mementos of other aspects of your life that bring you joy, such as collectibles and photos from your travels, furnishings that reflect your style and décor that is beautiful for those hours that you have to spend working. A home office can also be used for other interests such as scrapbooking, painting, photography or any hobby you might have, so make sure you keep this in mind as well. This is how the room can continue nourishing your soul.

Before

DIY Design
Stylish Bookcase

Are you looking for ways to give a generic bookcase a more custom look that makes a statement in your office or anywhere in your home? This project can be done on built-ins and also store-bought furniture that might require minor assembly. It's a great DIY designer facelift project we can do together.

Whether you have a built-in or freestanding bookcase, there are ways to personalize and update the style with some simple changes that don't cost a lot of money. Bookcases in a home office or any setting become a natural focal point on a wall because of their height. They are used to display accessories and many meaningful objects, so it makes sense to treat the furniture almost as a decorative photo frame for all your precious collectibles.

In this project, the bookcase was very dated and original to the home from the 1960s. Everything was white on white and didn't really make a statement in the space. It needed a facelift. Although I worked on this project with a unit that was built-in, the same ideas can be applied to freestanding bookcases that require assembly. In both cases, it's about giving a generic piece of furniture a more custom look.

By painting the backdrop in a different color from the frame and adding custom shelving and hardware, a regular bookcase can be transformed into a beautiful feature in any room.

Materials

Painter's tape

Bookcase—built-in or requires assembly

Foam roller and brush

Paint

Paint tray

3/16″ (0.5-cm) hardboard tempered panel (optional)

Panel board nails (optional)

Hammer (optional)

1″ x 12″ (2.5 x 30.5-cm) pine

Wood stain

Staining pads

Steps

1. Begin by using painter's tape on the sides of the bookcase to keep the paint lines clean and crisp. It's more effective when only the back has the pop of color to give the piece depth.

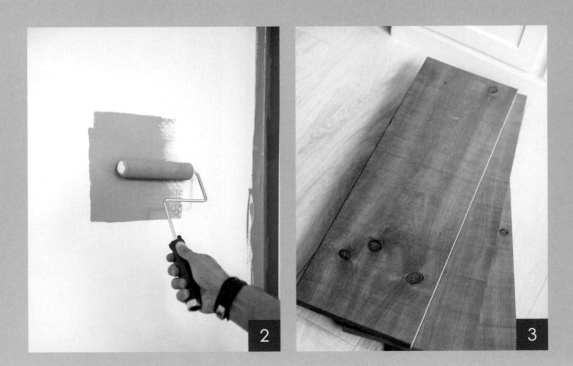

2. Cut in around the edges with the foam brush and use the foam roller for the larger areas until the entire surface is covered with paint. Once the paint dries, remove the painter's tape. If you plan to do this on a freestanding bookcase with a cardboard backing, I recommend that you replace it with a ³⁄₁₆-inch (0.5-cm) hardboard panel cut to size to the dimensions of the bookcase. You can attach it to the back of the bookcase with small panel board nails and a hammer. Applying paint directly to the cardboard can cause it to bubble.

3. Measure the bookcase opening and cut the 1 inch x 12-inch (2.5 x 30.5-cm) pine to the same width and depth. This will be your new shelving. Your local home improvement store can cut them for you. Proceed with staining a color of your choice with staining pads. I prefer to stain rather than paint because you can appreciate the wood grain. I chose a weathered gray to contrast against the white frame.

4. Replace the old particle board shelves with the newly stained wood shelves, and merchandise the bookcase with your decorative accessories.

After

The bookcase now has an updated style with simple cosmetic changes. Another option for the back is to apply self-adhesive wallpaper or use a stencil to add a pattern. If you have doors, update the hardware to refresh the look of the entire bookcase. Special thanks to Danny from Carved Woodworks for his help with this project.

Before

CHAPTER 8

Guest Bedrooms

An Inviting and Thoughtful Retreat Where the Details Make a Difference

Although the same principles of design that I wrote about in the Bedroom Suites chapter (page 73) apply to guest bedrooms, I wanted to create a distinction between the two when it came to decorating. I realize many homeowners might not have a spare bedroom they can dedicate exclusively to guests; the reality is it might be a shared room that has to perform other duties, too, like a home office, media room or more. In other words, the space is used by the family every day and then converts to sleeping quarters when company comes over to stay the night. Whatever the case may be, a smart design is essential to maximize the room's square footage for all your needs while creating a comfortable and inviting space for guests to feel welcome. It's like dual-decorating—for the now and for the future.

Spending money wisely is a conscious effort because guest bedrooms are usually last on the priority list for homeowners. It's understandable that if you move into a new home or are upgrading furniture in your current, you wish to spend your budget on the main areas used every day. What tends to happen is the "spare" or guest bedroom gets all the old furniture. It's a hodgepodge of the left-over pieces and hand-me-downs that you attempt to group together to form a bedroom set of sorts. Are you guilty of this? It's okay. Again, I understand. But, I also want to let you know that you don't have to sacrifice style for savings to create a retreat that you'll be proud to use as a home away from home for guests.

1 Walls

In a year-round guest bedroom, you have to take into consideration the range of patrons who might be staying in the room. I mention this because the décor and paint should appeal to both sexes. For example, I don't recommend pink or fuchsia walls with floral bedding if your in-laws are spending the weekend. It's best to look at the space as a hotel or bed and breakfast inn that everyone will be able to enjoy. The idea is to make your guests feel as comfortable as if they were on vacation—in your home—minus the valet parking and room service. What amenities do you look for when you go on vacation? It's the same principles behind decorating a guest bedroom.

The paint color inspiration can come directly from the bedding, which is typically the launching point for any bedroom design. Choose soothing colors inspired by scenes at the beach or nature, or take more risks with brighter hues of green, blue or yellow. Both can still remind you of a relaxing retreat in the Caribbean somewhere—it depends which island your imagination will travel to. If you prefer more exotic locations like Bali or Morocco, by all means bring that global experience into the guest bedroom, too. That being said, it is not necessary to add a rainbow of colors to make a room interesting. A monochromatic color scheme also works in a guest bedroom by using light and dark variations of one color to create harmony and a relaxing atmosphere. In the inspiration makeover, the walls were painted a light minty-green, but it had undertones of blue, which made the room feel light and airy inspired by a seaside retreat.

If your heart is not set on a color palette yet, you can save on paint at any major home improvement store by going directly to their "oops" section in the paint department. I usually begin here when budget is tight because quarts and gallons of paint have been marked down due to any number of reasons—anything from a wrong color match to a customer return. Who knows, but the point is that often times you'll get lucky and find a color that can work in your home. Instead of paying full price for the gallon, it's marked down to a fraction of the cost. It's a substantial savings when you compare paying on average $5 for an "oops" paint to $35 or more for a new one—of course, the prices will vary depending on paint brand and sheen. Be open to this because it can save you money right from the beginning when you decorate a guest bedroom.

Get Creative

Since guest bedrooms are usually not a space you use every day, you can have more fun decorating it and experimenting with daring paint projects. Transform a bland wall into a focal point by adding stripes that can easily be done with paint. It requires minimal time and materials because your existing wall color can be integrated into the design. In this makeover, I used quarts of paint in three colors—gray, teal and slate blue—to create depth while varying the width of the stripes. It's high impact for little money in this shared space, which is mainly used by the family as a media room for the kids; however, it can convert to a guest bedroom because the sofa is a pull-out sleeper.

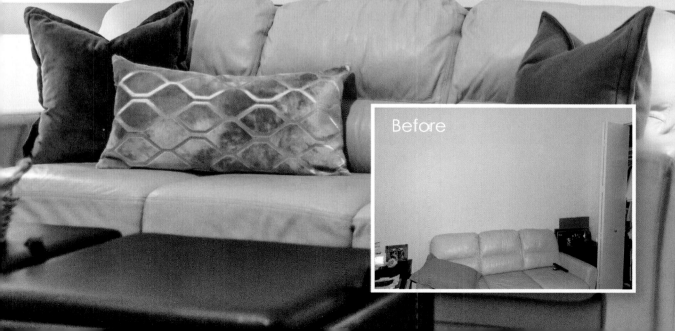

Before

Before

In interior design, stripes are used in a multitude of ways: horizontal, vertical and graphic patterns to complement any space. It's a great DIY project that you can do with painter's tape, a level to ensure the lines are straight and your favorite color of paint. The direction of the stripes can also visually alter the dimensions of the room. For example, horizontal stripes make a small bedroom look bigger while vertical stripes make a low ceiling look higher. You can do a mix of thin and wide stripes, tone on tone patterns or go bolder with the color choices to create one accent wall or a design that wraps around the entire room. The possibilities are endless. Stripes work in every decorating style from modern to country, so use your guest bedroom as a canvas for creativity.

Think "outside the box" for nightstand ideas that are budget-friendly such as using a unique chair, a stack of vintage suitcases or trunks, and even a small round stool.

2 Furniture

I don't want you to stress over not having a complete bedroom set to make your guests feel comfortable. The beauty is this room can have an eclectic design, and the furniture can be a select mix of old and new pieces. You don't need too much, but just the right amount to make the space inviting and functional.

In the guest room makeover, the bed frame belonged to the husband prior to him getting married, so it was technically his bachelor furniture. It was flanked on either side by two side tables that were meant to be used in a living room. This was evident by the low height, which would only work next to a platform bed. Ideally, nightstands should be flush with the mattress height or a few inches higher. It's a good height when it's comfortable to reach items while standing without bending over and it's much easier to raise your arms than to lower them while lying in bed, so keep these guidelines in mind to make sure the nightstands are functional.

In a similar scenario to the Bedroom Suite makeover, I softened the look of the room by going with an upholstered bed to balance the rest of the wood furniture. This bed was a steal at $450 for a king size, which I found in the clearance section. The lines were clean and modern, so it would appeal to both men and women, and the linen fabric was neutral and complemented the wall color. It looked expensive and luxurious like a bed at a boutique hotel.

In a guest room, it's nice to add furniture with drawers for company to take their clothes out of their suitcase, so I did that in the form of a dresser, chest and matching nightstands. It gave the bedroom a uniform style, so in this case, buying the coordinating set of pieces as a package deal was truly the best option to maximize the budget. However, don't feel the pressure to buy new furniture if the room is sparse with only a bed. You can improvise and use a chair or stool or stack of suitcases as a bedside table for an eclectic style.

Accent pieces that are easily movable around a room will make the space function better when it needs to convert to a guest bedroom.

When designing a shared space that also functions as a guest bedroom, two things are important when deciding on furnishings: scale and movability. In the media room, the side tables still work as traditional nightstands when the sofa converts to a sleeper. In the meantime, the glass top and teardrop turquoise base are design elements that don't take up a lot of room and complement the colors of the feature wall. Guest rooms function best when they don't appear cluttered. The last things guests want to feel is that they are sleeping in a storage room.

Where I was able to add the storage component was in the ottoman coffee table in front of the sofa, which had hidden compartments inside. It's a versatile piece in the media room to put your feet up, while storing board games and blankets; the lid switches to a tray for a more practical surface for drinks. However, when the room has to convert to a bedroom, the ottoman is on casters, so it can be moved out of the way underneath the window to make room for the sleeper sofa to be pulled out. This is what I mean by decorating a space for the now and for the future. As the host, you have to think ahead at how the room can accommodate guests in the easiest way possible.

I like using ottomans or benches in a guest bedroom because they are highly effective at elevating the wow factor as soon as you walk into the room. It transforms the bedroom into a mini-suite experience. They are also very practical as a spot for guests to sit or place down their luggage. Whether they take up the length of the bed at the footboard or a smaller version placed in front a mirror, I promise you it will get a lot of use—especially if the room doesn't allow for a separate seating area. Benches can be found at any discounted home retail store, so you don't have to pay full price.

3 Accessories

The accessories can truly make the guest bedroom experience memorable. These are all the touches that remind someone of home during their stay with you and, in my opinion, are even more important than the actual furniture to dress the space. Everyday items like linens, towels and soaps can be presented in a manner that reflects your hospitality and is a welcome comfort to your guests.

With the bed being the focal point of the room, the bedding is equally as important to create an inviting retreat. This is where all the accent colors and details come together that will make your guests feel special. Shop for high-thread-count sheets made out of cotton and plush blankets, and keep extra fluffy pillows on hand. Notice how I kept the same bedding that was on the old, mission-style bed frame, but it looks completely different when I mix new throw pillows and a coverlet to add layers on the bed. I used a white coverlet with gray pinstripes to contrast their existing comforter set with matching pillow shams. I love this look because I can fold back the comforter at the foot of the bed for a very luxurious touch. This is a great tip to refresh your bedding without having to buy a whole new set.

Throw Pillows

The throw pillows add color and a rich velvety texture in teal and cream, which is a calming color scheme inspired by the beach. Since the bedding already had a pattern, I kept them solid and simple. The combination of shapes in rectangles and squares adds enough visual interest without the need for any additional embellishment. It's a classic style that appeals to anyone who might be sleeping over on any given occasion. On the sleeper sofa, the throw pillows tie back to the colors on the striped wall. There's a subtle tone on tone pattern on the rectangular pillow placed next to solids, but notice how they don't detract from your eye going immediately to the feature wall. They support the color story of the room.

Lighting

There is an interesting story behind the ceiling light fixture in this room. It had a mini three-armed chandelier when I first saw the home, which was (1) the wrong scale, and (2) the design was too feminine. It felt like it belonged in a princess room. The best part was the new pendant lighting didn't cost anything because it was recycled from their living room where it looked out of place. Interestingly enough, even though the crystal orb fixture still adds a touch of glam in the bedroom, it's also a modern style that makes a statement. The scale is perfect to fill up the expansive space between the bed and the vaulted ceiling. This is no-cost decorating at its best.

I completed the lighting with glass table lamps on each of the nightstands that remind me of smooth sea glass. It's a translucent aqua color, and I love how the window light shines through it giving the effect that it's illuminated from within. The base is wide, mimicking the shape of the lamp shade, which balances perfectly the scale of the nightstands. New lamps are another way to refresh a tired-looking bedroom. They help to frame the bed and become part of the focal wall when you walk into the room.

In the media room, I used tall and skinny lamps to balance the 10-foot (3-m) high ceilings. It was also in proportion with the accent table, which already had a chunkier base. Had I used another lamp with a heavier base, the two pieces would've clashed, resembling more of a pedestal. Not good. I was also conscious of not adding a lamp that would compete against the striped feature wall. By keeping the base skinny, and the shades white, the lamp almost disappears. This is quite a difference from the lamps I used in the guest bedroom, which are a prominent design element.

Mirrors/Wall Art

Don't shy away from oversized floor mirrors because they can be dramatic in a bedroom, plus they are functional for guests to use when they get dressed. Leaning styles should be at least 72 inches (183 cm) tall for it to work. Anything shorter will look odd placed on the floor, so it's best to mount it on the wall. By going long and tall, you make a ceiling appear higher, similar to vertical stripes, and it's perfect for brightening up dark corners or adding depth and dimension to a room. By leaning the mirror against the wall behind the ottoman, it became the artwork in that area—no need to hang anything else around it to clutter the moment. A different position is behind a nightstand against a solid wall. It will make a modern statement and the room will appear larger.

The wall space above a bed can prove to be tricky finding the right artwork as you don't want to hang anything that will compete with the scale of the bed. I used three carved wood medallions to add warmth and texture. It was a simple detail to complete the focal wall. Other options include three-dimensional metal sculptures like starbursts or geometric shapes, wood panels and framed artwork. If your headboard is tall and dramatic, you might not have a need for artwork at all.

The artwork on the rest of the walls should be as generic as possible, so when company sleeps over they don't necessarily feel as if they are staying in someone else's bedroom. Imagine checking into a hotel room and seeing photos of other families everywhere—a bit awkward. The goal is to create an environment where your guests feel welcomed and that the room was prepared especially for their visit. When my partner's Italian family came to visit our home, I went as far as placing a framed photo of them on the nightstand. It was a memorable, personal touch that they appreciated after traveling so far from Europe to spend time with us during the holidays. I enjoy making people feel special through small details like this. A guest bedroom is a perfect opportunity to show your hospitality through thoughtful gestures that don't cost much, but say a lot and will have a lasting impact on your guests.

In the media room, which is a dual-purpose space used by the family daily and only converts to a guest bedroom when necessary, of course it's okay to personalize the space. After all, the primary function is for the kids to watch television and hang out and the décor should reflect how it's being used now. I created whimsical art by spelling out the kids' names with metal letters on the floating shelves, so they identified with this space. The clock is also a fun and functional element in the center of the feature wall. However, I was also conscious that the space would convert to a guest bedroom in the future during any extended visit by family/friends, so the cool part about the design is you can simply remove the letters to de-personalize the room and add other framed prints as artwork. The stripes make a modern and graphic statement, which works in either case as the backdrop for a media room or guest bedroom. The accent wall is completely interchangeable, which maximizes the square footage of one room for two completely different uses.

Welcome Basket & More

Creating a welcome basket that guests will appreciate when they stay over is something I enjoy doing. It's a detail that is personalized for their visit and very easy to make. You can buy a medium basket and fill it with bath towels and wash cloths, soaps, books/magazines for leisurely reading, bottles of water and some snacks in case they get a midnight craving. If they are not familiar with your city and plan on doing any sightseeing, I also like including brochures to different local attractions that might pique their interest.

I know this requires additional work to gather all the elements, but if you were the recipient of this basket, wouldn't you feel extra special? I can say that I relate to this experience with every makeover I complete; the most rewarding part is seeing the joy in the homeowners' faces when their room is transformed. A welcome basket will be practical, but we know there's so much more meaning behind it in terms of how you made the guests feel in your home.

Greeting them with an arrangement of flowers, a comfy robe and travel essentials are extra touches that create an inviting space in your home. Other ways to be a gracious host is to include an easy-to-reach charging station for phones and electronics; hooks on the wall and behind doors to hang their towels, jackets and clothes; room sprays; and an assortment of local postcards, stamps and pens on a table in the guest room. With such attention to detail it's a compliment if your guests won't ever want to leave!

Design Your Life

I believe we all have the power to make a difference in someone else's life no matter how big or small the act of kindness. As a host or hostess, opening your home to someone—whether it is family or friends—is truly a gift. You're providing food and shelter, which are basic human needs. The guest bedroom can be considered the equivalent of gifting someone a present that is nicely wrapped with a bow and greeting card. It lets them know that they are special enough for you to put forth effort into making the details and the presentation count. Consequently, it's a reflection of how thoughtful you are as a person to make sure their needs are met.

This has nothing to do with the need to impress—especially if you don't have a dedicated room solely for this purpose. In my own home, I have a sleeper sofa in the family room. And when family came over from Italy, we converted a home office into a bedroom with an elevated, inflatable guest bed supported by steel legs. However, I still made sure the bed was nicely made, the towels were laid out for them with travel toiletries and photos of Daniela, Fabio, Lara and Francesco were displayed in frames in the room and throughout the home. I did the best that I could with what I had, and it didn't go unnoticed. It made me happy to do that for them. The thought is truly what counts, and this is priceless for your guests—and you.

Before

DIY Design
Decorative Tray

Do you love the thrill of the hunt and bargain shopping? Thrift stores and flea markets are a great resource to find inexpensive antique mirrors. Let me show you how quick and easy this project is to make a decorative tray out of a framed wall mirror.

I love recycling mirrors and turning them into decorative trays. In a guest bedroom, it's an inviting detail you can place on the bed with a flower bud vase, some chocolates, a bottle of wine or magazines to make anyone feel welcomed in your home. It's inspired by boutique hotels, and you don't have to spend a lot of money to make their stay all the more comfortable and memorable.

Shop at thrift stores for a mirror of any shape that is big enough to use as a breakfast tray if necessary. The main thing to look for is that the surrounding frame be wider than 2 inches (5 cm). You need this room to drill into the frame and install the drawer pulls that will convert the mirror into a functional tray. The drawer pulls can be purchased at a local hardware store, or vintage pulls can be found at flea markets and thrift stores.

Materials

Framed mirror 20" x 20" (51 x 51 cm) or your choice of size

Measuring tape

Cordless drill

Drill bits

Drawer pulls—your choice of style

Self-adhesive vinyl bumpers

Steps

1. Turn the mirror over, so the backside faces up, and mark the center of the frame on opposite sides.

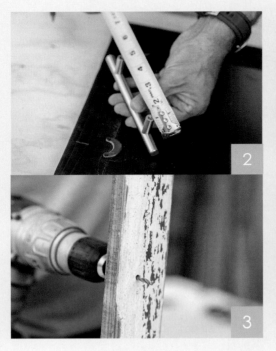

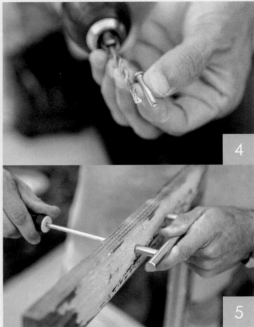

2. Measure the spacing between the drawer pulls and mark the holes centered on the frame.

3. Before you drill, make sure you have cleared the edge of the mirror. If not, you risk cracking the mirror. This is more obvious when you're drilling from the backside, which is the reason I began the project like this.

4. Drill the holes using a 5/16-inch (8-mm) drill bit. The size of the drill bit that you need will vary depending on the screws that come in the packaging with the drawer pulls. If the length is too long, you might need to purchase separate screws.

5. Install the pulls on the front and tighten the screws from the back. Now you have the handles to lift and carry the tray.

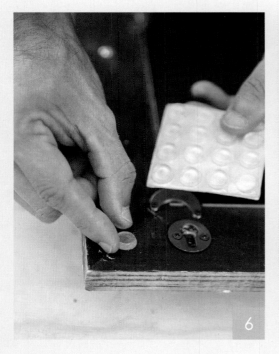

6. Attach vinyl bumpers on the backside four corners to prevent scratching any surface.

After

The decorative tray can be used in multiple ways in a guest bedroom: on the dresser, nightstand or en suite bathroom counter if you have the space. The project can also be done with smaller mirrors to place on a vanity. I like placing it on the bed when guests arrive with a bottle of wine and sweets to make them feel welcomed.

Before

CHAPTER 9

Multipurpose Rooms
Flexible Design Ideas to Maximize Your Square Footage

Multipurpose rooms are spaces in your home where different day-to-day functions are performed within four walls due to limited square footage. You probably have one, but you just don't realize there's a design term for it. An example that best represents this concept would be a studio apartment where literally one room has to function as a bedroom, living room, dining room and more. These space shortcomings don't just apply to building dwellers, it is also found in single-family homes where having a dedicated room to perform one task is hard to come by. In many homes, I find the family room takes the overflow and works overtime as a home office, playroom or more.

Although a living room and a family room might have similar furnishings, the main differences between the two are how they are used and its location inside the house. Living rooms are often in the front of the house and are considered more formal spaces for entertaining guests. Family rooms, on the other hand, are generally located in the back of the home and the style tends to be more casual for daily use by the family to watch television and hang out. Family rooms can also be considered dens, but regardless of how you describe it, I also realize not all homes have a spatial floor plan that will allow for this distinction. This is all the more reason why a multipurpose design will appeal to you.

The first step to creating a functional and stylish multipurpose room is defining zones within the space to perform a specific task. You have to compartmentalize the room into quadrants and decide how you wish to use each section; the second step is choosing furniture that will support the many uses and look great in different applications.

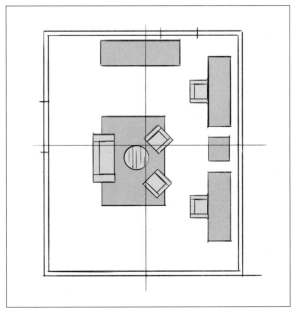

When a room has multiple uses, it's best to define the space into different areas depending on the task. In this layout, the room was used as a playroom, family room and home office.

1 Walls

Do you find yourself multitasking in one room? This means you're doing a bunch of different activities such as watching television, working online, snacking, playing games and more. I get tired from just thinking about it. The point I'm trying to make is this is where many aspects of your life converge in one room—like a highway—and, dare I say, the "traffic" shows in the disarray of the space. Wouldn't it be nice to do all that in an organized fashion that actually supports your lifestyle?

The challenge in the inspiration makeover was the young family was using this room as a place to hang out, work from home and as a playroom for the kids. Sound familiar? It was trying too hard to do too many different things and it showed by all the visual clutter. For a multipurpose room to be successful it has to have a cohesive design at first sight; yet it can adapt to different uses when necessary.

The first step was to address the walls by removing all the furniture from the room in order to start with a clean slate. In the other chapters I mainly discuss the topic of walls from a décor perspective, sharing tips to transform them as the first layer in the decorating process. Although the same ideas can certainly still apply to a multipurpose room (paint, wallpaper, molding, etc.), I want you to take a step back and look at the walls from a practical perspective. First, I want you to visualize how each wall can be used for a specific purpose that you need and second, how it will affect the overall look of the room. This is how we reorganize the floor plan to define the space into different zones—for working, playing and relaxing—using as an example the needs of this family.

A multipurpose room is more effective if you assign each wall a specific task because it allows the room to breathe and avoids overcrowding one area. This also leads to a better layout. Be aware of what task is assigned to the main feature wall and make sure you're okay with that being the focal point in the design. This is what I mean by how it will affect the overall look of the family room. In the makeover, the feature wall is where the brown sofa was located. I knew the homeowners needed a larger workspace, so I wanted to take advantage of the width for that purpose. It made no sense to define this wall as a zone for the kids because the first impression would be that you're walking into a playroom. With the feature wall defined to function as a home office, the smallest wall became the area for the children to do arts and crafts and organize their toys. This allowed me to create a cluster in the center of the room with furnishings for the family to gather. Many homeowners tend to push furniture all the way against a wall, leaving the center empty and resembling a dance floor. Don't be afraid to float furniture in the middle of the room, which frees up the wall space for other uses. In this family room, the space now features a multifunctional design that flows better and makes a statement. The gray paint color on the walls was never an issue. It was neutral and modern, so I knew I could make that work and not go through the expense of repainting the room a different color. What didn't work was the distribution of the furniture and how the room was being used.

2 Furniture

A sentiment I hear from homeowners is that they wish they had a bigger home. They feel that more space will alleviate a lot of their storage and organizing issues. In reality, I find that having more square footage will only create more disorder if you haven't taken control of your current situation. As an example, I've often encountered homeowners that feel the solution to their lack of storage is simply to buy more furniture. Yes, of course! Not. When you step back and look at the room, it's a warehouse of mismatched pieces swallowing up the space.

Design is about making the most use of what you have. In a multipurpose room, it's not only the floor plan that needs to perform different functions; so does the furniture to meet the needs of the family. Unfortunately, none of the existing furnishings worked in this makeover, so I had to start from scratch. This is where I spent the bulk of the budget; I was still able to save money by creating the look of custom built-ins for less and with pieces that do double duty within the space.

Workspace

I began with the feature wall, which I knew would be the area used as a workspace; however, I didn't want to use a traditional office desk, let alone two in the room since both the husband and wife needed separate work spaces. My vision was to create the look of expensive built-ins. I was able to do that by combining two consoles in a glossy, white finish framing a center cabinet. I repeated the consoles on either side to give the feature wall symmetry. The cabinet provides storage and organization with three compartments where you can easily fit a printer and any other office supplies. By going vertical with the cabinet we also took advantage of the ceiling height, which is always a good way to maximize a small space.

Storage units like this are modular pieces and can be configured in a multitude of ways to create a custom look on any wall. They require assembly and can be personalized with different door styles and frame colors. I primarily wanted the furniture to look beautiful without it being obvious that its main purpose was to function as a work space. What gave it away was the computer monitor on the left console. But even that becomes secondary when your eye has other beautiful things to look at in the room. The wife is a professional photographer, so I installed display ledges for frames above the consoles to complete the built-in appearance. Had I used mirrors or artwork on the wall above the consoles it would've resembled any other grouping you would see in a living room or entryway.

Fun Space

With the home office defined, I also needed to think of the kids in the design. I purposely made the arts and crafts zone on the left side of the room because it's not in immediate sight when you walk into the family room. Again, worth repeating, the feature wall is the main focal point. The small table set with chairs that once dominated in the center of the window is now tucked away in the corner. It's still useable space, but it's actually cuter because the kids have their own cozy and whimsical area to be artistic and have fun. What to do with all the toys? Well, this is where we also get creative and use a TV unit with open shelving to organize all the stuffed animals, puzzles and board games. Everything is accessible, but it encourages the children to put them away after they are done playing. This is another versatile piece that you can add doors to if you wish to create hidden storage. In the meantime, storage boxes can help organize smaller toy pieces or art drawings they work on.

At the moment, the family room is not being used to watch television, but you certainly have the option to do so by placing a TV on the media console in the future. It's a piece that grows with the family's needs and complements the overall look of the room. The colorful plastic table set keeps the kids' corner playful, yet the TV unit as bookcase/toy organizer is a piece all members of the family can use.

Sit & Gather

The priority for this family wasn't to have a large gathering space in the family room because they can accommodate that in their living room. This is the reason I kept the scale of the furniture smaller because it was more appropriate for a sitting room or den floating in the center of the room. Their original bulky brown leather sofa would've completely overcrowded the space. I kept the fabric neutral on the settee, so that all the furnishings blend with the overall color palette. This helps create a cohesive design between the different zones in the same room. When creating a grouping in the center of the room, clean lines and a low back work best, so that it doesn't close off the space. If the furniture is too tall and blocks the sightline to other pieces around the room, then it's a good sign it's not the right fit. This still applies even if the room was larger.

Great Room

There's a misconception that if you have a bigger room, then you won't have as many decorating issues. This is totally not true, because when you have more square footage to decorate it's even more challenging to come up with a unique furniture layout that is not repetitive throughout the space. You find this a lot in a great room, which is its own form of a multipurpose room, whereby a living room and family room is shared space. Within this larger floor plan you still have to identify zones for having a conversation, watching television, working, entertaining and more—whatever the needs are for the family—similar to a smaller room.

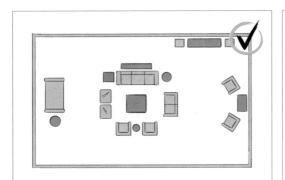 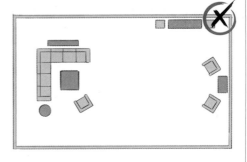

Furniture arrangement can be just as tricky in a large space as in a small room. In a Great Room, create different groupings that relate to each other, yet stand apart as their own cozy area.

In a great room the best way to divide the area visually into cozier zones is with the furniture placement. Depending on how large of a room, you might be able to create two or three groupings that relate to each other within the same space, yet might be used in different ways. If you chose two, you have to balance the visual weight of the furniture between the two groupings—meaning you can't have a large sectional on one side of the room and then two small accents chairs on the other. The symmetry will be off; with three arrangements, you can offset the distribution by beginning with a cluster in the middle, which helps to anchor the room, flanked by smaller conversation areas on either side. In this great room, the music area is defined by the piano and a modern chaise; the main furniture grouping is in the center defined by the hanging pendant lamp; and then there is a smaller sitting area with two chairs off to the right side.

The furniture arrangement in the middle of the room provides enough seating by combining two leather armless chairs with a coordinating sofa; to break up the matching set and introduce another texture, I added two floating ottomans opposite an elegant, exposed wood-frame sofa with scrolled arms. I love these pieces together because they feel collected through the years, expressing the homeowners' individual style.

It was difficult to find a coffee table within budget that was the right scale for this large area and that could relate to all the surrounding furniture. The solution was to make our own with four garden stools and a glass tabletop meant for a dining room. Super chic and eclectic for much less.

Upholstered dining chairs are more stylish as desk chairs and the coffee table also doubles as storage for toys to keep the space organized.

Double Duty

In the inspiration makeover I needed chairs for the desks to make the workspace functional; I also needed additional seating in the middle with the settee. I knew I didn't want to overcrowd the family room with too many chairs, so choosing two that could be multifunctional was ideal. I found them with these upholstered wingback-style chairs. It added style with a subtle geometric pattern and brought in a hint of blue into the color palette. They are comfortable when pulled up to the desk for working, but equally beautiful across the settee to complete the grouping. The chairs really exemplify the definition of a dual-purpose furniture piece. Chairs, like ottomans, are a good choice for shared spaces because they don't interrupt the traffic flow into other areas and keep the room visually open. Although minimal in scale, you achieve more impact in the room by using two.

The round coffee table is also a versatile piece that doubles as a storage basket for throws, toys and even books and magazines. The white also ties in with the built-in cabinetry, maintaining a cohesive look in the family room.

3 Accessories

Family rooms tend to be spacious, so the accessories should be proportional to the size of the room or else they get lost. This means if you're placing objects on a shelf or hanging artwork on the wall, make sure they can be appreciated from a distance since, more often than not, you're dealing with an open floor plan. Of course, it's about achieving the perfect balance between small, medium and large items.

Although we are creating different lifestyle zones for individual tasks, the accessories help tie everything together throughout any multipurpose room. You achieve this by keeping the fabric choices and color palette consistent or else risk dividing one room into mini-spaces that don't relate to each other visually. On the settee, I used striped throw pillows that complemented the colors of the accent chairs, wood finish of the cabinets and an area rug. The modern color palette is very consistent with neutral beiges, creamy whites and cool blues accented with black. In the great room, the style is more traditional. I pulled the accent blue from the area rug to give the room a pop of color against the warmer wood tones. At first glance it simply reads as one beautiful space, and ultimately, this is the goal. The different uses aren't necessarily meant to be obvious.

The iron chandelier hung above the coffee table defines the central seating arrangement.

Mixing accessories in different sizes on open shelving feels more collected through the years.

Lighting

Lighting can be used as a way to define a zone as well. The best example of this is in the great room where an oversized pendant hangs above the coffee table, catching your eye immediately as you walk into the room. Although large in scale to balance the size of the furniture grouping, the hand-forged iron frame keeps the area open. If you have different zones to light in a multipurpose room—in addition to the main light source coming from the ceiling—be cautious not to go too lamp crazy. Mix different styles and sizes of table lamps with architectural floor lamps, and fabric and metal shades. In the family room, I used two tall lamps with a black and gold drum shade to dress up the console. They make a statement in the room during the day and provide accent lighting at night near the designated play area in the family room.

Wall Art

You can control where the eye is drawn in a multipurpose room with wall art. Whether it's a painting or framed prints, the scale will determine how much attention it will receive in the room. Group smaller frames together to make a bolder statement and vary the size of the wall art throughout the room to make it visually pleasing. In the family room, the collection of portraits displayed above the desk consoles personalizes the area and allows for a rotating gallery of photos. I also mixed the frame colors to make them pop against the gray paint color.

Before

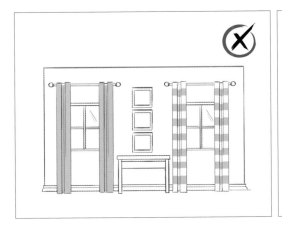
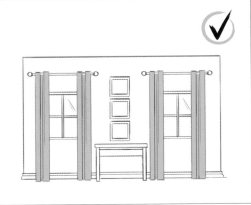

In an open floor plan, window treatments should be consistent to unify the different spaces—especially if there is more than one window on the same wall.

Window Treatments

In a shared space with an open floor plan surrounded by windows and patio doors, I often get asked if the window treatments should all be the same. My answer is yes and no. This is truly on a case-by-case basis as it relates to your specific layout. The decisive factor is whether you have windows and/or doors that are on the same wall shared by both spaces. If so, keeping the same curtain panels would be best. However, if the windows and/or doors are on opposite sides of the room, then you can justify a change—with some additional guidelines.

For example, in this dining room and lounge setting, the homeowner had sand-colored panels on the sliding doors leading out to the patio from the dining area; however, in the lounge setting, I decided to use mocha-colored panels for the window. This works because (1) the curtain panels in both areas are the same style, (2) it's most effective when you use a darker or lighter version of the same color and (3) the window and sliding doors are on opposite sides of the room and not on the same wall. This is the correct way to create a subtle separation of spaces within an open floor plan. It would be a mistake to use a pattern or bolder color because the switch would be too dramatic and not blend with the overall look of the design. In case there's any doubt, the curtain rod should always remain the same throughout for consistency in hardware.

Design Your Life

Living an organized life is not that difficult if you incorporate smart storage solutions into the design. This is important in all rooms, but even more so in a family room to maintain a clutter-free environment. It might be helpful to think of the room as an office where life—in this case day-to-day business—needs to run efficiently and smoothly. Designate an inbox for every member by using decorative photo boxes or file-folder caddies that can be displayed on a shelf if you don't have room inside a cabinet.

Bookcases and entertainment centers can become cluttered with photo frames, souvenirs picked up during your travels, books and DVDs. At least twice a year (spring and fall), edit the collectibles, place photos in albums and donate items you no longer use. Less is more on shelving, so highlight the most meaningful things. Incorporate decorative storage cubes for each of the kids, where they can easily store a limited amount of toys and games in the family room. The overflow can go back to their bedroom, and the cubes can be lined up against the wall as part of the room's décor.

Other details that will make a difference is having a decorative box on the coffee table to hide remote controls that end up getting lost, coasters on the side tables for drinks, and go as far as wrapping neatly any tangled cables and/or cords that are visible behind the TV or lamps with a cable tie. These are all things that eventually will become a routine, so you're able to keep the area neat and tidy to enjoy spending quality time at home with your family.

Before

Gallery Wall

Wouldn't it be nice to turn cherished memories into artwork that enhances your home décor? Together we can create a gallery wall that tells the story of your life in a few simple steps.

Often times I see photo frames scattered everywhere throughout the home—and especially in a family room. On a coffee table, side table, crowding shelves on a bookcase—anywhere there is a surface you usually find a mismatch of frames. I completely understand every moment captured in time has meaning, but when it comes to displaying them all in your home, it can overwhelm the room to the point that you truly can't appreciate any of them.

The best way to feature your beautiful photos is to create a gallery wall. It becomes a focal point in the space that complements the design instead of cluttering it. Depending on how many family pictures, you can dedicate an entire wall for this vignette, or a section of a wall, but the idea is to highlight them in one area, which becomes part of the room's décor.

There are different groupings you can create using a combination of shelving and accessories to tell the story of your lives through the display.

Materials

Scissors

Craft paper

Pencil

Transparent giftwrap tape

Measuring tape

Painter's tape

Level

Hammer and nails

Decorative shelves

Photo frames—different sizes

Typography wall art

Cordless drill

Steps

1. The best way to visualize the grouping on the wall before you hammer any nails is to cut out the outline of the frames and décor with craft paper. Do this for the different frame sizes and use a pencil to mark the location of the picture hanger on the paper.

2. Proceed to hang the craft paper shapes on the wall with a giftwrap tape until you come up with a layout that is pleasing to the eye. You can be as symmetrical or as scattered as you want—as long as the display looks balanced. There are two different ways to do this:

For a scattered design, mark the horizontal and vertical center of the wall and use painter's tape to draw axis lines as a reference. Make sure you also take into account the height of any piece of furniture that will be placed on the wall. Hang different paper shapes within the quadrants, beginning from the center out to the sides, and distribute the visual weight between the diagonal sections.

3. For a symmetrical display, use painter's tape with a level to create an oversized square or rectangle on the wall. Align the outer edges of the frames with the grid border. The spacing and frame sizes can vary inside the grid as long as the edges line up forming the outline of a larger frame. Feel free to move around the shapes in both display options (scattered and symmetrical) until you come up with a final arrangement you like.

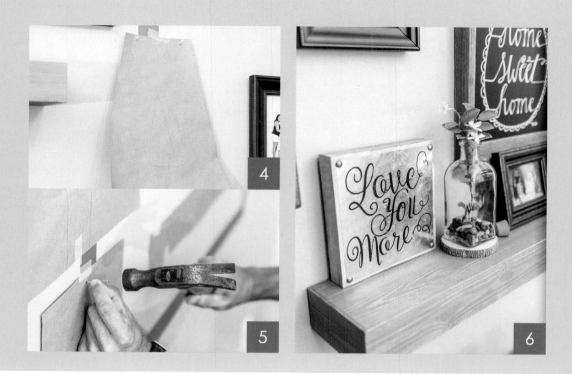

4. Leave spacing for any signage in between the frames. You can visualize this directly on the wall by using the craft paper shapes, or if the item is lightweight, you can place it into the arrangement temporarily using a giftwrap tape.

5. Once you like a layout, mark the location of the picture hanger onto the wall through the craft paper with a hammer and nail. This is where you will hang the frame.

6. Finally, complete the display with shelving to add more depth to the installation. This is a great way to mix and match frames, but create a unified style. It also lets you lean frames up against the wall and add other accessories as part of the collection.

After

Time is precious and goes by quickly, so I love how the gallery wall is now a beautiful display of special moments in my family's life. The collection is meaningful and makes an artistic statement in the home.

Before

CHAPTER 10

Outdoor Rooms
Create More Living Space and Add Value to Your Home

Cooking barbecues, roasting marshmallows and playing on the swings are just some of the outdoor activities we all enjoy doing, and some of the fondest memories can take us back to our childhood. It reminds us of a simpler moment in time where the setting played a key role in the happiness we felt as we played in the backyard or local park. I believe we continue to relive those feelings every time we gather at home with family and friends for cookouts and more when the seasons permit us to do so. As an adult, we are passing on that joy and tradition to a new generation.

It kind of makes you look at your outdoor space differently, right? It's the scene for many beautiful memories to be made, but homeowners are sometimes at a loss not knowing how to decorate this area. The simple answer is to treat it as you would any indoor room. Whether it's a courtyard, patio deck or terrace, if it's empty then you're truly not taking advantage of valuable living space and experiencing what entertaining alfresco has to offer.

There are a few things to consider when designing an outdoor room. Depending on the size of the area, you have to decide if you want a place to mainly sit, a place to eat or maybe a combination of both. Once you determine how you wish to use the space, the next step is defining the areas for that very purpose and selecting furniture to create the same function of a living or dining room that you find inside the home. The only exception in the decorating process is that your choices have to take into account durability since they are exposed to the elements in Mother Nature. Luckily, there is a wide selection of outdoor furniture styles, so you're not limited to plastic, foldable tables and lawn chairs. In my world, this is only acceptable if you're camping.

1 Walls

It's nice to step outside and be surrounded by nature. It's a totally different experience than sitting in a sunroom constructed of insulated glass walls with doors and windows or a screened-in porch, where instead of glass you have screen walls and doors. These spaces can certainly be beautiful and give you the feeling of being outdoors, but they are still enclosed and attached to the home.

When designing an outdoor room, the walls can have a literal or figurative meaning depending on the ideas you're implementing. In some cases, the courtyard, deck or patio terrace is connected to the home, so literally some of the exterior walls of the structure need to be addressed in the design concept. Additionally, you could use planting materials and architectural details to surround the outdoor space with "green walls" in a figurative sense, which creates a setting that feels like your own secret garden.

The courtyard makeover is a perfect example of how addressing the walls first completely transformed this area from a blank slate into a beautiful room. There was hardscape everywhere, from the pavers on the floor to the concrete walls of the home, so the goal was to soften the appearance and add more greenery. I couldn't plant anything on the ground since all areas were covered with pavers, so I had to get creative. The solution was to install artificial boxwood hedge panels on the largest wall, which became the backdrop for the outdoor room. The lifelike foliage panels require very little maintenance, which was important to the homeowner. It's made from a premium plastic that is able to withstand extreme weather without fading or cracking. Instead of covering the entire wall I decided to create three panels to mimic the architectural look of molding you would see inside a home. I could've used real climbing vines in planters along the wall that can grow tall on trellises, but (1) it wouldn't give me the instant coverage I needed for a one-day makeover and (2) natural plants require water and pruning, which was not conducive to the homeowner's busy lifestyle. This was really the best solution for the clean and modern style of the courtyard.

The artificial hedge panels are available in mats, rolls and expandable lattices. They also come in different foliage and flowering varieties, including ivy, ficus, lavender and more, so it's a great way to add privacy and instant greenery in a very affordable way. This is a material apartment dwellers can consider to dress the railings of their balconies, too. I know some view artificial plants as a big faux pas, but there are exceptions depending on the application. In the courtyard, the ivy was used in a similar fashion to wallpaper to add visual interest on a blank wall as part of the backdrop in the design. This doesn't mean I support the use of artificial plants inside your home. Small greenery as an accent on a shelf or table is okay, but you're not fooling anyone with a potted tree in the corner. They usually become dust collectors.

In an outdoor room, there are other ways to build focal walls where there were none to begin with, especially when you are not limited by ceiling height. In the Bali-inspired makeover, the wood plank wall became an architectural feature and blocked the view of the neighbor's house. I know this might be a more time-consuming project, but it's still doable in one day by securing 4 x 4-inch posts into the ground with quick-setting cement mix and attaching the wood planks horizontally. You can stain or paint them on the same day. The goal is to create a beautiful structure in your yard with this design idea, but it doesn't necessarily mean you have to construct an expansive wood wall either—even small sections only 4 feet (1.2 m) wide will do the trick.

Trellis panels, known for their open lattice framework, can also be used as decorative walls in the ground or in a planter. They are available in different sizes at any home improvement store and can be used alone as an accent piece or with climbing vines to surround a patio or deck. Other natural materials I've used in makeovers are bamboo, reed and willow twig fences. They come in rolls and you can use them to create a decorative panel or cover an unattractive porch ceiling or chain-link fence. The texture can give a tropical feel to your backyard or garden—like you're on vacation in the islands. The advantage is it can also be used as a privacy screen from your neighbor, so it's a twofold effect.

For many homeowners, lack of privacy can be a big deterrent from fully enjoying their outdoor spaces. The initial solution would be to consider installing a fence. There are many styles and materials to choose from, ranging from wood to vinyl, but it can be quite expensive. In addition, you will still have to blend this expansive wall of fence along your property line into the landscaping. As a designer, I try to find decorative solutions to costly problems. Speaking purely from an aesthetic perspective, my suggestion is to use hedge plants to create a "living wall" along your property line or closer to the deck or patio terrace. With patience and time, these shrubs and plants will eventually grow tall, creating a more intimate space for gathering in your outdoor oasis, plus you'll address the privacy concerns. I recommend that you visit your local garden center and talk to a landscape expert to learn about the various species of hedges and trees that grow well in your area.

If your property is barren from any green walls, at least now you know different ways to help Mother Nature.

2 Furniture

Wouldn't you love to have a place to drink coffee or read a book, especially when the weather is nice and cool? There is a true sense of freedom when you're outside. You're not confined to any walls that might block your view of the garden. As you design this special moment for yourself, realize that the furniture can be as chic and comfortable as your interior spaces; this means a beach chair is not what you should be considering as you furnish this area. I chuckle as I write this, but you just never know!

The patio furniture is how an outdoor space starts to transform into a room. The best use for the courtyard was for casual entertaining and gatherings by the family, so the furniture selection was similar to a living room grouping comprised of a sofa and two conversation chairs. Yes, it's a set from the same collection and that's okay. I know it's opposite of what I suggest buying when you're furnishing an indoor space, which is to avoid a matching set of anything. However, outdoors I actually like it when the furnishings coordinate because it helps to unify different areas you might be decorating to give the exterior a structured, well put-together look. I think if you start mixing and matching too many pieces there's a chance it will resemble a hodgepodge. Trust me on this.

Furnish an outdoor space in the same manner that you would an indoor room. An all-weather sectional, dining set, throw pillows and area rug will ensure that it's beautiful and durable for many seasons.

There are many beautiful styles to choose from, such as wood, aluminum, all-weather wicker, wrought-iron and more. You should consider the look and function and the durability based on weather conditions. I chose a brown, rust-proof, cast aluminum frame to tie in with the home's window shutters. The slats across the top of the coffee table give the appearance of wood, but without the maintenance. The sofa and chairs are deep and comfortable and come with the cushions, which are weather-, mildew- and stain-resistant for lasting durability. This is important since the fabric is exposed to different climate conditions for use season after season. The material of the furniture must also be taken into consideration. In direct sunlight with no shade, a cast aluminum material might get too hot to the touch for daytime use, so it's something to keep in mind.

Another popular finish is the all-weather or synthetic wicker. In the past, the word wicker was associated mainly with country or traditional decorating, but you see this texture done in a much sleeker way and in darker shades of chocolate brown/espresso to work in modern homes. Wicker and rattan are often used interchangeably, but wicker refers to the style of weave, whereas rattan refers to the actual material made from a naturally growing vine-like species. By going synthetic, the furniture is more lightweight, durable and eco-friendly.

In the Bali-inspired makeover, I used a combination of love seat and two chairs plus a dining set with four chairs to define two areas underneath the same terrace. You can see how keeping the furniture style consistent helps to unify the look of the patio. As when shopping for a dining room or living room, make sure to take measurements of the outdoor space to ensure you're buying patio furniture that will fit. If you have a small space or balcony, a bench or a small bistro table will look just as nice. Look for styles that stack or fold for easy setup and storage like campaign chairs that mix wood and canvas or teak and wrought iron. There are also balcony-height table and chair sets so that you can enjoy the view over the railing.

Yet another popular patio style is wood, but the right type can make all the difference. Teak is considered the best because it's a strong hardwood that is beautiful and durable. It can last up to 50 years, whereas pine or cedar furniture will have to be stored in the winter season. The disadvantage is any wood can absorb moisture leading to rot, mildew and mold so you have to take care of it. Teak will eventually turn a grayish patina if not sealed every year.

In the same manner that we have to maintain the inside of our homes, an outdoor area is no different. With any patio furniture, some form of upkeep is required to maintain the looks and durability. No matter the finish or fabric, eventually dirt and the natural elements will take its toll on the surface. If it's not realistic to store your furniture in a garage or shed during the winter, there are ways you can preserve it by using furniture covers and pavers. The covers come in many sizes and shapes, which prevent water from standing on your furniture; the pavers help raise the legs so they aren't sitting in puddles, which can lead to rotting. Even though the fabric on the cushions might be all-weather, you can prolong their look by spraying them with a stain and water repellant. It is still recommended that you bring them inside or place them in a storage deck box when not in use. I know some of these ideas are not convenient or the most attractive, but it's a way to protect your investment so you can enjoy your outdoor spaces for many seasons to come.

Before

Bang for Your Buck

Patio furniture can be sold in individual pieces and in sets. You can get more bang for your buck by buying a set that includes a sofa, a couple of chairs and coffee table; separate the furniture pieces to decorate more than one area. In many cases you can use the sofa and coffee table as one grouping and then use the two chairs with an accent table in between to create a smaller seating arrangement somewhere else. This is how you can stretch your decorating dollar until you're ready to purchase more pieces to add to your outdoor collection.

Areas around a pool deck should also be considered in the design plan. I love the look of resort pools and use that as inspiration by placing a couple of chaise loungers with an accent table in between for sipping cocktails while relaxing. This is where you can get a bit more eclectic and not have the accent tables necessarily "match" the main furniture grouping. For example, I like using ceramic garden stools as tables. They can withstand the sun and rain and are versatile pieces because they can also be used as additional seating. It's a fun way to add a pop of color.

Bring a global style to your outdoor setting with accessories such as lanterns, sculptures and bamboo textures that create an exotic retreat in your own backyard.

If you want to enjoy the crackling glow of a fire and entertain guests around a bar, don't think having one custom built is your only option. Portable fire pits come in many styles and provide another cozy gathering space in your outdoor setting. Surround the fire pit with comfortable Adirondack or arm chairs in the same material that match your patio furniture. The same applies to the bar and barstools. Considering accent furniture requiring minor assembly is easier on the budget and will look great on your patio. You can find storage bars made for exterior use that are lightweight with features such as a wine glass holder, plus you can also use them as a buffet while entertaining. Gazebos, hammocks and swing chairs are other great additions that can bring comfort and a whimsical style to your outdoor retreat, maximizing your living space in nature.

3 Accessories

Do you need curtains, rugs and throw pillows? Of course! I said from the beginning it's the same concept as decorating a room inside your home. These are truly finishing touches that will turn any exterior space into an outdoor room in every sense of the word. They can be styled with lanterns, planters, textiles, dinnerware and décor—even exterior lighting and artwork. It could be that your home is missing this crucial third step if you find you're not being inspired to spend more time on your patio, deck or balcony.

Cabana-Style Panels

I love the look of private cabanas at the luxury hotels! You can create a similar style by hanging outdoor drapes around the opening of covered terraces to frame the view onto the pool or garden. There are many fabrics to choose from, including light and airy sheers, energizing stripes, solid colors and versatile patterns, that you can coordinate with any color scheme. If you like an exotic style, bamboo panels can add a global influence. The texture is 100 percent natural and each panel is trimmed with a 1-inch (2.5-cm) fabric border and hangs from rust-resistant rings. If privacy or shade is not an issue, then you only need to hang one panel on either side of an opening from a decorative outdoor rod. In the Bali-inspired makeover, I used these panels to soften the look of the columns on the covered terrace.

On the same topic of exotic flair, I love thinking outside the box and coming up with unique ideas that have a big impact. For example, over the loveseat I placed mosquito netting, which typically you would see as a canopy hanging over a bed. It's a minimal cost for the dramatic look! It creates a romantic enclosure and transports you to a fantasy destination.

Area Rugs & Throw Pillows

An outdoor area rug is great for hiding or minimizing unsightly floors, but the main purpose is really to define a furniture grouping and tie the color scheme together as another layer in the decorating process—in the same manner we use it indoors in any room. Most of the styles are made of 100 percent polypropylene, which is easy to clean, and are fade and mildew resistant. In our inspiration outdoor room, I used a 5 x 8-foot (1.5 x 2.4-m) area rug of artificial turf. It was modern, yet unexpected, and worked well to add a green and soft texture over the pavers and ground where the new furniture sat. It's durable and a fun surprise.

Yet another form of floor cover you can use is wood deck tiles. They are available in many styles, sizes and colors, ranging from real wood to composite material. The installation is quick and easy because they interlock and float directly on the floor to cover unsightly concrete on a patio or balcony. They are a perfect solution for small spaces and can also be used as area rugs to define furniture groupings since the tiles are modular. If you're feeling creative, you can even create the illusion of an area rug with paint directly on your concrete floor or deck. Use two colors to frame the center with a contrasting border.

Choose decorative throw pillows with the same weather-resistant properties. It can add a pop of color on the patio set that might otherwise come with a neutral seat cushion. In the loveseat under the mosquito netting, the different accent pillows against the back make the setting more inviting. Mix and match different patterns on your outdoor throw pillows in the same manner as a living room sofa. They are stylish and functional layering pieces and can be used to unify different groupings throughout your patio, so the color scheme is cohesive throughout the many areas.

Potted Plants

Even if you don't have a green thumb, it's nice to add natural greenery and color to help soften the look of the hardscape—be it on concrete or a wood deck. Add flowers and foliage in pots and containers with lots of color to brighten the space and group them in clusters of different heights for more impact. These ideas also apply to urban dwellers that might have a balcony or small patio as an extension of their living space. You can't have an outdoor oasis without natural plants in your surroundings. I know it takes a bit of work to water and maintain, but it's worth it for the ambience they add.

Water features like ponds and fountains add a soothing sound in your garden.

Loungers around the pool create a resort-style experience steps from your home.

If you need a crash course in Gardening 101, there are two popular categories for plants: annuals and perennials. Annual plants have a life cycle that lasts only one year, which means they need to be replanted once they die. The advantage is most annuals bloom for a long time and are less expensive. Perennials, on the other hand, can live for two or more years. They return year after year, but their blooming periods are shorter. I actually love mixing the two in containers, but if you're still at a loss and don't have a green thumb, check with your local garden center to see what plants grow well in your region and take notice of the planting beds around your neighborhood.

Outdoor Oasis

Umbrellas are also a must in an outdoor setting. They reflect that resort lifestyle when placed next to chaise loungers around a pool or in the center of a dining table; they also provide necessary shade from the sun's rays.

Incorporate other decorative touches to create a space that appeals to all the senses, such as fountains, wind chimes and oversized hurricane lanterns with candles. FYI, they make flameless outdoor candles, too, that won't melt in the sun like traditional wax. I also love using a string of twinkle or globe lights across the ceiling or around the trees to enhance the mood of your outdoor retreat just steps from your home. You want to make sure the patio looks great during the day and at night, too.

Outdoor throw pillows add a pop of color on patio furniture.

Clusters of candleholders create the perfect ambience when entertaining in the evening.

Entertain in Style

When the time comes to fire up the barbecue or cozy up to a warm fire there are ways you can use gardening elements for entertaining guests. For example, a plastic plant container makes a great ice cooler! They come in many sizes and colors, and it's a unique way to keep beverages cold at your next party. Smaller flower pots can be used as flatware caddies at a buffet station, and terracotta plant saucers can become decorative plate chargers as part of your table setting. Cute ideas, right? Remember to elevate the dinnerware from paper plates and consider acrylic or melamine plates and beverage cups, which are better for the environment and come in many designer styles, too.

All these elements combined will help you create the perfect outdoor room to enjoy all season long, adding valuable square footage to your home's floor plan.

Design Your Life

There's a saying that nothing in nature is perfectly symmetrical. There is never a straight line. Boulders are round, mountains are wide and trees expand their branches in all directions. Nature is beauty in its simplest form. Yet sometimes we forget this gift is free for us to enjoy every day and we don't stop to literally "smell the roses" in the hustle of everyday life. I'm guilty of this too. Creating a sanctuary outside allows you to take a moment to reconnect with nature. It doesn't require a major landscaping project to make a perfect setting. Define a small area where you can place a hammock or bench with a small accent table next to it. This becomes a peaceful retreat where you can close your eyes, feel the breeze and reenergize your spirit.

I find that when I step outside and look toward the back of my home from this different perspective, I also gain a deeper appreciation for what I have and for what I work so hard to maintain . . . a piece of the American dream. I know it sounds silly, but walk into your yard as far away from the structure as possible and then look back for a moment. We identify with our home's curb appeal so much because we drive up to it every day and walk through the front door. The back view is almost taken for granted. Yet it's just as important as the front and back cover of a book because within the rooms, like pages, the story of our lives has unfolded. I found this reawakening by taking the time to fully enjoy my outdoor space. Like our home, it becomes an extension of us.

Before

DIY Design
Candle Fixture

Do you love dining outdoors underneath the romantic glow of candles? It feels very European, like staying at a Tuscan villa that has a beautiful cobblestone patio. There is nothing wrong with letting your imagination travel to faraway places as you create a scene in your home that reminds you of these special moments. Together we can bring a bit of rustic charm to an area above a dining table that might be missing a focal point.

Similar to a dining room, where a beautiful light fixture hangs above the table, you can also create a focal point in an outdoor setting over a patio table with a unique candle fixture. It can be fun and rustic or whimsical and functional all in one.

At one point during my many shopping sprees for a makeover, I saw a ladder used in a home store display hanging from the ceiling and loved the look. When I came across this random wood ladder used for bunk beds that someone threw away in the dumpster, I was inspired to make this project. Yes, you can even find great materials to repurpose as home décor by going dumpster diving! You might be laughing, but it's so true. Look for garage sales listed in newspapers or drive around your neighborhood when bulk trash pick-up is scheduled, because someone else's trash can be salvageable and used in a DIY project. I've done this a few times already and, for obvious reasons, it's very cost-effective.

With the ladder being free, I spent minimal materials on mason jars, rope and hardware. This project works best when you have an architectural structure to hang the fixture above a table, like a pergola or gazebo. However, the mason jar candleholders would also look nice hanging from tree branches or a shepherd's hook lining a pathway. No electrical outlets are needed since we are using candles to illuminate the area at night.

Materials

Black spray paint

Screw eye rings

⅛" (0.5-cm) quick links

Wood ladder

Cordless drill and drill bits

Black link chain

Cutting pliers

Mason jars

Natural twisted sisal rope

Scissors

Votive candles

Decorative filler

Candle lantern mason jar lid

Steps

1. If your screw eye rings and quick links are a different color than your chain, you'll need to spray paint them to match, so set them out with the spray paint in a well-ventilated area. If you prefer the look of stainless steel, buy the chain in the same finish.

Spray paint the screw eye rings and quick links black to match the link chain. I screwed the eye rings into a piece of scrap wood, so that I can paint all sides at the same time.

2. Attach the screw eye rings to the four corners of the ladder by drilling a pilot hole first. For this project, I placed them 18 inches (45.5 cm) from the ends of the ladder to balance the length. This is subject to change depending on what is best suited for the ladder size you are using.

3. Attach the link chain to each of the screw eye rings using the quick links and tighten. Make sure to leave the link chain long by 2 feet (61 cm) to have enough slack to cut down to size.

4. Connect a 12-inch (30.5-cm) section of the chain from opposite sides and use another quick link to secure them together creating a double loop. Repeat for the other end of the ladder and cut off the excess chain using the cutting pliers.

5. Attach screw eye rings to the structure parallel to where the chain meets the ladder. Determine how high you wish to hang the candle fixture and cut a new section of link chain to length. Secure above with a new quick link and attach the bottom to the same quick link used in the double loop. Make sure you have enough clearance between the table and the bottom of the mason jar that will hang from the ladder—between 30 to 34 inches (76 to 86 cm).

6. Replace the standard lid on the mason jar with a candle lantern lid that features an open top connected to a matching chain link. Hang mason jars with sisal rope at different lengths across the ladder for a rustic look. Tie a double knot on each end and cut the remaining rope with scissors. Votive candles are really inexpensive, so if you wish to use real candles it will be more realistic, but always keep safety first in mind and make sure no portion of the rope is near the flame. A safer option is flameless candles.

7

7. Decorate the bottom of the jar with filler such as small pebbles, dried moss or glass. These supplies, along with the mason jars, can be purchased at any craft store.

After

The old ladder turned new candle fixture will definitely be a conversation piece the next time you're entertaining. When not used with candles, you can put fresh flowers, air plants or succulents, so it becomes a living installation in your outdoor room.

Acknowledgments

There are many people to thank that have been a part of my journey to get to where I am today. On television programs, although I'm the face viewers mainly see, I always point out there is a team of camera operators, producers, editors, makeup artists and more behind the scenes that collectively make the final product possible that you see on the air and enjoy at home.

I believe the same applies to life. There has always been a team of people that supported my dream along the way and had a direct influence on the opportunities that led to my personal and professional growth. First and foremost, I wish to thank my family. My mom, dad and my brother, Marcus, have always been there for me. My dad taught me all the DIY skills I know, and my mom is my biggest fan, recording all my shows—dating back to VHS tapes—from day one. They have shown me what unconditional love is and accepted me for who I am. I thank my grandparents for having the courage to leave behind their native Cuba to start over in the United States in search of a better life for them and consequently, for the generations that came after. They taught me what hard work and dedication is, and the opportunities I have today are because of their sacrifice. They are my Guardian Angels in heaven now. Thank you to my partner, Robert, for being by my side and seeing me become the man I am today. A big thank you to my extended family, uncles, aunts, cousins and relatives, for being my cheerleaders; and, to all of my childhood and lifelong friends for supporting me in every way, with special thanks to Johanna, Claudia, Jenny, Leticia, Mariana, Gloria and Mercy. In particular I have to highlight Carmen, who always knows how to make someone laugh. She influenced my love for decorating by seeing her create beautiful spaces in her own home. I admire you and I will always be your handyman with my toolbox ready to hang anything you need.

My career path took many twists and turns, but there have been defining moments that changed the course of my direction. My dreams began to come true early on as a teen in the entertainment business, by first working as an actor with Cindy from Stellar Talent. Thank you for believing in me. As I began to make the switch into broadcasting and interned at a local Telemundo station, I want to say thank you to Maria Cristina Barrios and Tatiana Riquelme for giving me my first opportunity to be on-camera talent on a program. I learned how to edit and produce, and I gained invaluable experience on what it takes to make a television show. I'm forever grateful to Alice Jacobs at WSVN for being the first to "green light" my pitch for a design segment and giving me a platform on television. Thank you for seeing my vision and for changing my life. While I was at WSVN I was blessed to meet and work with Jorge Rodriguez, who was my "MacGyver" on every shoot, assisting me far beyond his role as cameraperson, and where I was assigned my first segment producer Diana; twelve years later my chapter

ended at WSVN with producer Lauren. A huge thank-you goes out to Bert Medina for having a direct impact on my career twice: first, for allowing me to make the cross-over into Spanish-language programming with my design segments, and years later for the opportunity to launch a weekly program on WPLG. In Spanish-language media, I thank Vanessa Pombo and Maria Lopez Alvarez for the chance to work as the designer on a weekly makeover show for five seasons and decorate the sets for special projects on the network; Mari Garcia-Marquez and Richard Borjas for letting me share my decorating ideas on the morning show; and Armando Correa at *People En Español* for featuring my work in the pages of the magazine. Special thanks to Adamari Lopez and Toni Costa for entrusting me with designing Alaïa's nursery, which has been one of the most important projects in my career. I'm grateful to the marketing team at ION Television for developing the ION@Home content and for supporting my work. Thanks to Robin Sheingold, Katie Sammon and Chris Addeo for searching for me to be their host and the entire production team I get to work with throughout the year. To the many producers I've worked with, I respect and admire your talent. Teamwork makes the dream work. I also want to thank the team at Eatman Media Services, Ross Eatman and Todd Foos, for their support, and to my college friend, Mari, who made the introduction many years ago.

Many of the room makeovers in this book were a part of my weekly program in South Florida, so I thank the entire WPLG Creative Services team and my *So Flo Home Project* crew for making the content that I share with readers possible. Special thanks to all the wonderful homeowners for trusting in my work and whom I've had the privilege to get to know as I decorate their homes. I also appreciate the design collaborations with many talented people who helped make my vision for a space a reality. Among them are Danny at Carved Woodworks, Peter from TurfTech Pros, Cinthia, Ben from Chalk & Brush, Frank from Landscape Rehab, Steve from TurfWorx, Ron from Accent Closets and Martha Rodriguez from Ideal Baby & Kids. The beautiful photographs in this book I owe to Venjhamin Reyes—thank you for your talent and time revisiting my design makeovers to capture all these images for the reader to enjoy; and to Andrea Centeno for the illustrations. Special acknowledgment goes to photographer Hector Torres for granting me permission to use the images of the nursery I designed for Adamari Lopez.

I still can't believe I can add the title "author" to my credits thanks to Page Street Publishing and the amazing creative team that believed in my book concept. Thank you to Sarah, Will, Meg and everyone else on the Page Street team for making my dream come true. I visualized publishing a book one day, but I didn't know when it would happen. I'm grateful that my journey crossed paths with Sara Bendrick and it led me to you. Thank you to Sarah and Page Street Publishing for the opportunity to accomplish a lifelong goal that had eluded me in the past. If there's one life lesson I've learned in this amazing career, it is to trust in God's timing.

Thank you to each and every one mentioned here for allowing me to live my passion—and for the many others that I'll meet in the future that will continue to shape my career. I will cherish this book forever as a time capsule of this special moment in my life. Someone, please pinch me.

About the Author

MARTIN AMADO is a TV personality, interior decorator, lifestyle expert and contributing writer on the subject of home décor. He can be seen as the host and designer on *So Flo Home Project*, airing Saturday mornings at eleven o'clock on WPLG Local 10, an ABC affiliate in Miami, FL, where he was born and raised. Prior to that, South Florida viewers became familiar with his work on the home makeover segment 'Room for Improvement" that aired on WSVN 7 News, FOX affiliate, for over twelve years. He is currently host of branded content on ION@Home, seen nationally on ION Television network, and is a design contributor to Un Nuevo Día, Telemundo's national Spanish-language morning program.

His past work in the general market includes hosting HGTV's *Small Space, Big Style*, as guest designer on various episodes of HGTV's *Decorating Cents* and working as an on-air guest expert for the HGTV Home brand on the Home Shopping Network. In addition, Martin has worked on numerous Spanish-language media platforms in the United States and throughout Latin America such as Galavisión, where he was the lead designer on *Decorando Contigo*, which aired for five seasons; his decorating segments have been featured on the FOX Life network (formerly Utílisima) on programs such as *Tu Vida Más Simple* and *Hogar Express*; and three webisode series as a brand spokesperson: SaturDIY: Moen Makeovers, Hogar Chic and Baño Chic. He has also contributed decorating and lifestyle tips in the pages of *People En Español*, *Latina Magazine*, *TV y Novelas* and *Vista Magazine*.

He works exclusively with clients through his home styling company, The WOW Factor!, Inc., where he specializes in one-day makeovers and working with a minimal budget to achieve the decorator look for less! Please visit www.martinamado.com for more information.

Instagram: @martinamadotv
Twitter: @martinamadotv
Facebook: Martin Amado: Home Décor & Lifestyle Expert
Youtube: Martin Amado

Index